rhĕ′torĭca®

A toolkit of 21 everyday writing techniques

Scott Keyser

RETHINK PRESS

First published in Great Britain 2016
by Rethink Press (www.rethinkpress.com)

Book Mark

Approved by
Plain English
Campaign

Cover by Phil Cleaver & Kay Kim, t.r.u.

Mind Maps® is a registered trademark of the Buzan
Organisation Limited 1990, www.iMindMap.com

For Annie, Oliver, Seth and Alice

ACKNOWLEDGEMENTS

My publisher, Lucy McCarraher, and her trusty editor, Joe Gregory, of Rethink Press, have not only guided this book to completion, but have also supported me when the going got tough.

Andy Maslen, my partner in our eight-year training collaboration, Write for Results, helped me re-discover the richness of the English language and its power to persuade.

Christopher Trevor-Roberts, my inspiring (and inspired) Latin and English teacher, gave me an understanding of the building blocks of language and how to use them. He also imbued in me his love of language and learning.

Many minds far greater than mine have written about persuasion and language — no less than Aristotle and Cicero in ancient times, to the more modern spirits of EB White, William Strunk, Mark Twain, Stephen King, John Humphrys, Melvyn Bragg, James Borg, Sam Leith, Dr Robert Cialdini and Lynne Truss, to name but a few. I owe them much for my nascent understanding of this wonderful, vibrant language of ours.

Anne, my lovely wife, showed her usual tolerance of my machinations and her pragmatic attitude to the various hurdles I had to overcome in writing this book.

Thank you all.

Contents

SECTION II: Drafting 63

SECTION III: Editing

Introduction

Words have power.

Words can inspire, excite, anger, disgust, seduce, hurt, heal, arouse, enrich, connect. They move us from one state, condition or behaviour to another.

Words can break cement.

Pussy Riot, Russian feminist punk group

Amnesty International supporters write letters to political prisoners around the world, giving them hope and comfort in the face of the worst abuses. Their words show solidarity with the cause — and save lives. Sack-loads of cards and letters arriving at prison gates are a sign to guards and governments that the world is watching.

Words express our thoughts, feelings and ideas. If we can't share them with others or make them come true, they might as well not exist. They're merely cells in the creator's brain that fire, then die. Shooting stars on the head of a pin.

Any big idea you care to mention was given life through words. Democracy would not exist if its first advocates hadn't found the words to communicate the concept. Government of the people, for the people, by the people would have remained a dream of the ancient Greek imagination.

And what about rhetoric, or the art of persuasion? Our ability to use the written word to persuade someone to do something they would not otherwise do is a life skill. Aristotle, the grandfather of rhetoric, described it as a *tekhne* (art, craft or skill, hence 'technical' and 'technique'). That's why, for centuries, rhetoric — alongside grammar and logic — sat at the heart of Western education, before the misguided educationalists of the 20th century removed it.

The skill of written persuasion is one that I've spent most of my working life studying. Through training thousands of corporate employees around the world in writing skills over the last 12 years, I've identified 21 persuasive writing techniques that can transform writing overnight.

These techniques form the rhetorica® method of persuasive writing and the 21 chapters of this book.

WHO IS THIS BOOK FOR?

If you are…

- a student writing an essay, thesis, résumé/CV or Personal Statement

- a consumer making a complaint or trying to get a refund on a faulty product

- an inventor or entrepreneur seeking funding for an idea

- a business owner or employee struggling to write an email, report or blog

- a charity worker seeking sponsorship

- a single parent persuading a municipal authority to house you

- a home owner writing to a neighbour about a party wall dispute

- an English teacher wanting a 'refresher' (we won't tell)

… then this book is for you.

The techniques demand no special level of intelligence, education or knowledge of grammar. You can apply them the moment you've learnt them. And as with any skill, the more you use them, the more effective they will be. And, in case you're wondering, it's grammatically OK to start a sentence with 'And' – despite what you were told at school.

HOW IS THIS BOOK STRUCTURED?

Simply. It follows the three steps of the writing process: plan, draft, edit.

That may sound obvious, but I see many people trying to do all three at once: they start drafting without planning, develop their thoughts as they go and do some half-hearted editing. Then they hit a roadblock. 'Maybe I should have taken a different angle… Mmm, I don't know as much as I thought about my reader, or this topic. I wonder if I should speak to someone else about this…' They down tools and start planning properly, but they've wasted precious time.

Fail to plan, plan to fail.

Anonymous

PLANNING

Planning is the most neglected part of the writing process, yet it offers three benefits:

1. Speed: you save time in the form of fewer drafts and no re-writes.

2. Effectiveness: you get the results you want.

3. Confidence: you feel in control of the process.

Section I of this book delivers those benefits by walking you through the five elements of planning.

DRAFTING

Only when you've nailed your plan should you start drafting. And your job here is to just get the text down, fast. This is your raw material; it will be rough and ready, with gaps and place-holders, but if you've planned properly it will be a good start. Section II of this book adds 12 powerful drafting techniques to your writing toolkit.

EDITING

When you've done your first draft, then you pull on your editor's green eye-shade and start editing and checking it. Section III covers four professional editing techniques that will turn your first draft into powerful prose.

rhetorica® will show you how to get your reader to do what you want them to do. It may only take one well crafted sentence to convince your reader. This is not about using fancy words or parading your mastery of grammar and punctuation. This is about getting the results you want through the written word.

If, after reading this book, you'd like a more interactive experience in improving your writing and adding some more tools to your writing toolkit, consider joining my online programme, rhetorica® Online (www.writeforresults.com).

In the meantime, I hope you enjoy this little book and I wish you well in your writing.

SECTION I:
Planning

Give me six hours to chop down a tree and I will spend the first four sharpening the axe.

Abraham Lincoln

rhetorica® Technique #1:

Write For Your Reader

Sounds simple, doesn't it? Don't be fooled. It takes effort and emotional intelligence.

Like any activity, performance is influenced by mindset. And most writers adopt the wrong mindset because they focus on the wrong thing. Themselves.

Most readers — like most clients — are more interested in themselves than in you.

The more you mirror their self-perception, the more you appeal to their self-interest, the more persuasive your writing will be. I call this being 'reader-centric'. Until you get this, you'll struggle to change their mind or their behaviour. That's why writing for your reader is Technique #1. It's a *meta* technique, because it supports and informs the other 20 techniques of the rhetorica® method.

Being reader-centric calls for an emotional shift on our part. We have to change our focus. Here's what I mean:

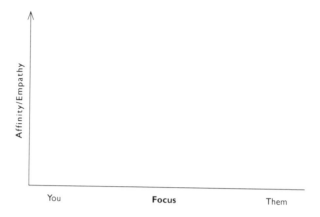

The *y* axis is affinity/empathy: making your reader feel understood and connected with you. Empathy is defined as the capacity to understand and share someone else's feelings and ideas as if they were your own, to feel *with* the other person. Empathy creates connection. Another related word here is *rapport*: the ability to connect with others in a way that creates a climate of trust and understanding.

The *x* axis is our focus as the writer: we can choose to focus on ourselves ('You') or the reader ('Them').

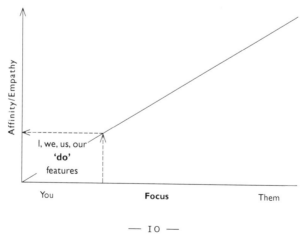

You can see that when we focus on ourselves, use words like *I, we, us, our, do* (e.g. 'what we plan to *do*') and talk about the *features* of our product, service or argument, the connection with the reader is weak.

But when we shift focus to the reader, something magical happens. Our language changes. We automatically use the magic words *you* and *your*, the powerful word *get* and our content centres on the benefits to the reader of our product, service or argument – which is what they're most interested in. And your language is not the only thing that changes: you'll also find that the *structure* of your communication reflects your new reader focus. The connection with the reader is strong, as you can see below.

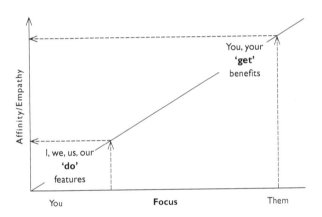

The mistake most writers make is to focus on themselves and their agenda; after all, that's dead easy to write about. But like the party bore who only talks about themselves and shows no interest in others, most readers find that a turn-off. The irony is that the more we focus on the other person, the more interesting they find us.

SO HOW DO WE GET TO KNOW OUR READER?

We can do 'live research': go and speak to them. That's easy if they work in the same place as you. But if they don't, call them, visit one of their shops, speak to someone who knows them, read their blog, Google them, look them up on LinkedIn, or go to an exhibition/conference they're attending (but try to avoid hanging around outside their home late at night; that's stalking).

If they're still as elusive as the Scarlet Pimpernel, then you must use one of the writer's key skills — your imagination.

Have an imaginary conversation with them:

- 'What sex are you?'

- 'How old are you?'

- 'What do you do?'

- 'What do you want more of/less of?'

- 'What are your values? What motivates you, gets you out of bed in the morning?'

- 'What are your fears, hopes, dreams and aspirations?'

Your goal here is to think your way into their heads, walk a mile in their shoes, see the world from their perspective, understand what makes them tick. By building a pen-portrait of them (referred to in content marketing circles as their *persona*), you can write in a way that engages them and makes them receptive to your message.

Another way of expressing reader-centricity is 'personalisation'.

For me, this is more than tailoring or customisation: it's about being so tuned into the reader that they recognise themselves and their agenda in your words. That's powerful.

THE MAGIC WORD(S)

When I talked a few moments ago about shifting focus to the reader, I said that something magical happens. You start using the personal words *you* and *your*. These are magic words, because they make the reader feel as if we are talking to them as an individual. They satisfy a basic human need to be heard and feel special. Using them liberally is a simple device that's almost impossible to over-do.

(Grammar Geek note: *you* in this context is the second-person singular, as opposed to the first-person singular, which is *I*.)

If you have any doubts about the power of personalisation, consider this: if you happened to spot your own name — the ultimate personal word — in a piece of writing, would it make you more or less likely to read it? (See how many times I used the Magic Words then, by the way: did it make you feel uncomfortable or strange? It works because it's how we naturally communicate with each other.)

When addressing multiple readers in the same document, like a magazine article or an all-staff memo, inexperienced writers tend to use *you* in a plural phrase (technically known as the second-person plural); you'll see this a lot in emails, too. They'll use phrases like 'some of you' or 'all of you', as if their readers were huddled around one copy of the document. When I see phrases like that I look behind me to see who else is in the room reading over my shoulder!

> *Do not address your readers as if they were gathered together in a stadium. When people read your words, they are alone.*
>
> David Ogilvy, a great copywriter and
> founder of advertising agency Ogilvy & Mather

The word *audience* is another symptom of this disorder.

When I train people in writing skills, I often hear them say, 'I'm writing for my audience'. But there are five problems with this word:

1. 'Audience' suggests people are listening (the Latin root of the word *audiare*), but — despite the fact that there *is* an auditory aspect to writing — our readers read our words.

2. 'Audience' is too broad. It lumps all our readers into the same bucket, implying they're all the same, which of course they're not. It fails to take account of individual emotional, cultural or intellectual differences. It also suggests we're broadcasting our message in the hope some of it lands, rather than personalising it to individual readers or reader-types. It's the difference between 'broadcast' and 'narrowcast'.

3. Audiences tend to be passive. Picture an audience in a theatre or cinema: they sit passively, taking in the spectacle. The traffic tends to be one-way. Good writing should feel more like a conversation than a lecture.

4. Audiences don't take decisions; individual readers do.

5. Finally, when you read something do you feel like an 'audience'? No, of course you don't. You feel like *you*: a unique, special, distinct individual and you want to be addressed that way.

6. You're writing to an audience of one — your reader.

These gents are not about to give each other a 'Glaswegian kiss'. They're Uighur horse dealers in a market in provincial China agreeing a deal. While you might not be selling horses, you want your readers to feel as connected to you as this.

FOOD FOR THOUGHT

1. Pick a recent document where you were trying to persuade a person or an organisation to do something.

2. Count the number of times you used the words *I, we, us* and / or the name of your own organisation, team or department.

3. Count the number of times you used the words *you, your* and/or the name of the reader's organisation, team or department.

4. Now compare the two numbers. If the total in 2. is bigger than the total in 3., your document is *author-centric*. If it's the other way round, it's *reader-centric* — which is the way to be!

The bottom line: the more your reader feels connected to and understood by you, the easier it will be to persuade them to do what you want them to do. Emotionally intelligent writers understand that good writing is not about them, but about their reader.

rhetorica® Technique #2:

Set Time Aside To Plan

Imagine you're about to drive somewhere.

You've parked on a slope. You switch on the ignition, press the accelerator pedal and release the hand brake. If you time it right, you pull off uphill rather than sliding downhill. Moments before you release the hand brake and set off, however – especially if you're over-revving – the engine starts to whine as it strains against the retaining force of the brake.

Like the engine, inexperienced writers strain to start drafting, because they want to see visible progress. Good writers, on the other hand, take their foot off the gas and keep the brake on, at least for a while.

Whenever I have something substantial to write — especially if there's time pressure — after all these years I'm still tempted to release the brake, put my foot down and start drafting. I call this an 'action-illusion': it makes me feel busy, but in the long run it's neither efficient nor effective. I get halfway through my draft only to realise that I'm going in the wrong direction. Kicking myself, I delete the draft and start again. That's a 're-write' and, in terms of efficiency, a disaster. From bitter experience I know that when I draft without planning, I regret it.

The single biggest problem I see in non-creative writing is poor or non-existent planning. So your first *practical* step on the path to Planning Heaven is to set time aside to do it.

Before you start thinking about your reader, researching them and the topic, consulting colleagues, organising your thoughts, establishing the content and structuring it, you need to ring-fence planning time. But how much?

If the box below represents the total amount of time available to produce the whole document from start to finish, what's the *minimum* proportion of that box that you should spend planning?

Here's my recommendation:

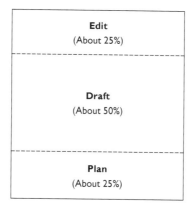

If you only have four *minutes* to produce an important email (to a client, your boss or a jilted lover), spend at least a minute planning (we'll look at what that means in the next four techniques), two minutes drafting and the last minute editing, checking and proofreading.

If you can devote four *days* in total to the document, then allocate one day to planning, two days to drafting and the final day to editing, checking and proofreading. What I'm talking about here is not elapsed time, but total time spent working on the document.

If you're producing a document with other people (e.g. a bid or competitive tender), then it's even more important you respect the 25/50/25 principle. As a team you need to agree when your planning stops and your drafting begins (and when your drafting stops and your editing begins). The best way to do this is to work backwards from the final submission/publishing date and set deadlines for each of the three activities.

Ring-fencing your planning time, imposing this constraint on yourself, will give you focus. If you don't set a limit on it, planning can expand into the time available and before you know it, you've run out of time to draft and edit your document – which is a disaster.

Where 25% is the minimum, I'd set the maximum at about 50%. Any more than that and you run the risk of not giving yourself enough time to draft and edit.

Of course, these proportions are only a guide, but they're better than nothing. In my experience most people lack discipline when they plan. They start drafting too soon, get halfway through the document before realising they've spent time on an unnecessary section, topic or aspect, or gone down a blind alley, or found gaps in their knowledge. But by then it's too late; they've wasted precious time. And that's the price you pay for poor or non-existent planning.

So if you often write under pressure of deadline and *speed* is an issue for you, paradoxically you need to spend some time planning. That will mean you produce a better first draft, with less editing and no re-writes.

FOOD FOR THOUGHT

1. Think about a document you need to produce in the near future. The more important it is, the better.

2. Set a deadline for it, i.e. when do you need to send/publish/issue/submit it? Then make a realistic estimate of the *total* amount of time you will spend on it. Allow for inevitable interruptions and delays.

3. Calculate 25% of that total time. That's your (minimum) planning allocation.

4. Now *diarise* that time, either in one chunk or several. Commit to planning, and only planning, in that time. Consider those diary entries as sacrosanct.

The bottom line: remember the old cliché 'Fail to plan, plan to fail'? Make planning a deliberate, conscious, structured activity by setting aside a specific amount of time to do it properly. Treat it as an immoveable commitment. It will pay off in the form of better first drafts, less editing and no re-writes.

All of which gives you three major benefits:

1. Speed — you save precious time;

2. Effectiveness — you achieve your communication goal;

3. Confidence — you know what you're doing and where you're going.

(I know I'm repeating myself from the Introduction, but it's so important that it bears repetition.)

rhetorica® Technique #3:

Nail Your Message

In December 2014 I ran a short survey on writing skills. 92% of the respondents said the aspects of their writing they'd most like to improve were 'clarity and impact' and 'expressing complex, technical ideas simply'.

There's a sequence here.

Simple language aids clarity, and a clear message – if it's relevant to the reader – delivers impact.

But why is clarity elusive?

For me, it starts right here, with planning. Clarity starts in the head, not on the page. Amateur writers jump straight in to drafting and rely on that process to clarify their ideas. While I recognise that drafting can *sometimes* help to refine an idea, avoiding planning altogether is not clever, because that's where we get clear on our main message. Clear writing reflects clear thinking.

However technical or complex your document, you need to be able to 'nail' your main message(s). For several years I've trained general field engineers in writing skills. This has included showing these highly qualified oil & gas technicians how to craft one-page abstracts for technical papers. Despite not understanding most of the content, however, I can spot from a hundred paces when the author has nailed the problem that the project will address and/or the project's objective... and when they haven't. Here are some examples of clear messages:

Problem/Opportunity	Objective
Staff attrition (43%) is higher than the industry average	To cut staff attrition by 14% within 18 months
We've developed the first generation of driverless cars, but surveys show that 65% of people polled don't trust them	To convince the general public that driverless cars are safer and more reliable than human-driven cars
Oil production in the XYZ field has fallen by 20% in the last three years	To find the root cause for plummeting production in the XYZ field over the last three years
Teenage pregnancies in Townsville have risen by 35% in the last three years	To cut teenage pregnancies in Townsville by 50% by the end of the year

My experience with technical writing (e.g. law, engineering, audit/accountancy, architecture, IT consulting) is that the main messages get lost or buried in the undergrowth. Good writers unearth the message, scrape the mud off and buff it to a gleam *so that the reader gets it in one go.* I call this 'nailing your message' with a single, summary or 'topic' sentence that opens your communication. Subsequent paragraphs should then prove, describe, support or expand on that topic sentence. It might look like this:

The objective of this project is to cut teenage pregnancies in Townsville by 50% within three years.

We will achieve this by:

- *taking a road show into local schools to talk about safe sex and the impact on life chances of falling pregnant while in school*

- *making condoms freely available in every school and college*

- *setting up an online forum for teenage mothers to share with their peers their experience of having a child*

- *offering a signposting service to sources of help, advice and support*

Outlining your main message in a single, opening sentence makes it stand out and draws the reader's eye to it. More importantly, it gives them a mental framework to understand the ensuing detail.

THE CLARITY BELL

You may find this odd, but clarity gets me emotional.

When I'm planning a piece of communication, I grapple with it. While the process I follow (i.e. the one I'm writing about in this section) is structured, my mental activity is messy and chaotic. I'm sparking with different ideas, exploring different avenues and options, hypothesising different scenarios. My mind is agitated. The research is often tedious, progress uncertain; sometimes all I have to show for a planning session is some doodles and notes. But eventually a pattern of understanding emerges and I begin to see a path through the forest.

Maybe that's reflecting what is happening in my brain at that moment: the neurons have settled on a synaptic pathway, excluding all others. My mental agitation subsides and I get an overwhelming feeling of calm and peace. And that's when the emotion hits me. Relief, joy, excitement, anticipation – I'm not sure which it is, but my body tells me when clarity is present.

In NLP (Neurolinguistic Programming) terms, I'm quite a kinaesthetic (emotions, feelings, touch) person, but your dominant sense may be sight, hearing, smell or taste. What does *your* clarity look, sound, smell, taste or feel like when it hits *you*?

Planning any activity can be challenging. It can feel like you're spinning your wheels. So the risk of getting frustrated and jumping to drafting is huge. But you need to resist that urge. Give your mind the time it needs to triage the information that will clarify your message. That's why ring-fencing dedicated planning time – ideally over several days to allow the unconscious mind to work on it while you're asleep – is vital (see Technique #2).

HOW DO WE MAKE THE CLARITY BELL RING FOR YOU?

Planning is an abstract activity. It involves gathering and analysing data, thinking hard, exploring options, talking to people, using our imagination. In neural terms, it's a high-order function, which demands more mental processing power than something more visible, like drafting or editing. So the more we can engage the body in planning and make it more physical (and more *fun*), the likelier we are to do it. Here are two tips: verbalisation and Mind Maps®.

VERBALISE: SAY YOUR THOUGHTS OUT LOUD

Research conducted in 2014[1] at two German universities into the neural activity of creative writers when brainstorming threw up an interesting finding (the italics are mine):

'... expert brains showed increased activation... in several regions associated with speech production. Taking these findings together, they paint a picture of expert creative writers: ideas bubble up within them, already on the road from concept to expression, readily communicable, *almost rising into their throats.*'

I'd go one step further and suggest that we can help the writing process by expressing (literally 'pushing out') what's in our throats. We can make the leap from idea to expression by verbalising our thoughts. It's as if we're speaking them into existence.

I regularly ask myself, *aloud*, 'What am I trying to say here? What's my main message?' Then I answer it out loud. (I talk to myself a lot when I'm planning. I know: I need to get out more.)

But this works because it turns my abstract thoughts into audible words that either ring the Clarity Bell or they don't. It's binary. Try it for yourself and let me know how you get on. At the end of the day, you must find what works for you.

MIND MAP® YOUR WAY TO CLARITY

I'm a self-confessed mind mapper.

Developed in the 1970s by Tony Buzan, Mind Maps® are a powerful, 'whole brain' technique that allows you to capture a lot of

---

1 Erhard, K, Kessler, F, Neumann, N, Ortheil, H, & Lotze, M (2014). Professional training in creative writing is associated with enhanced fronto-striatal activity in a literary text continuation task. *NeuroImage*, 100, 15–23 DOI

information on one page using pictures, colours, words, shapes, symbols, lists and numbers.

Published with the kind permission of Jayne Cormie, of The Thinking Business

To plan any major document or communication, I get out my magic markers and a large piece of white paper or card and settle myself down on the sofa in my office. I start playing with ideas, using the naturally associative tendency of the brain to trigger more ideas.

In the centre of the paper I create a picture of the topic and start drawing lines radiating out from the centre like the branches of a tree, with each branch a different colour. These thick, central branches represent high-level ideas. So if I was mind mapping this book, there might only be three central branches: one for each of planning, drafting and editing, like this:

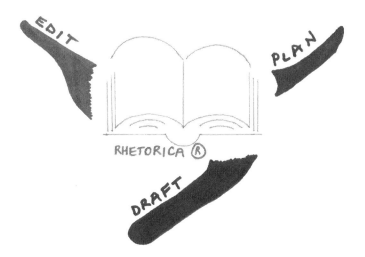

Let's say I got on a roll, brainstorming the subject of planning. I might come up with lower-level ideas that would sit on the 'Plan' branch, adding them as thinner branches to show the hierarchy, like this:

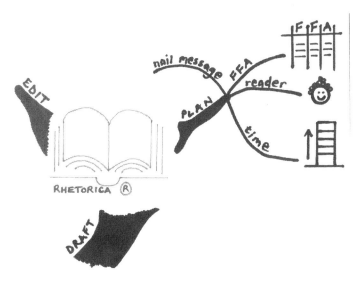

As you can see, it's rudimentary and I'm not the world's best draughtsman, but that doesn't matter. I'm capturing ideas with words and pictures as they come to me. The beauty of Mind Maps® is that you don't have to stay on one branch at a time: you can jump about from one topic or sub-topic to another, following your thoughts. By mirroring the brain's associative thinking process, it frees up your natural creativity. And it captures the output of brainstorming on any subject.

Externalising on one page what you know about a subject and grouping it meaningfully gives you a map of that subject — but a map that includes mountain ranges *and* the contours of individual hills. It gives you the fine grain and the broad sweep. That combination of big picture and detail makes it much easier to see the whole territory and pick the messages that will most resonate with your reader. In fact, more often than not, when I mind map a piece of communication, the main message naturally falls out of the exercise. The Mind Map® makes it explicit and obvious.

WHY ARE MIND MAPS® SO POWERFUL?

Because they mimic the human brain.

We don't think in straight lines or sequences like a computer, but in an organic, multi-dimensional, radiant way where one idea or stimulus sparks a number of associations, which in turn trigger more ideas and connections, and so on.

This radiant structure reflects many structures in nature – from our own bodies (e.g. our hands and limbs) and central nervous systems to the branches of a tree or the petals of a flower. It's no coincidence that a brain cell ('neuron') resembles a Mind Map®:

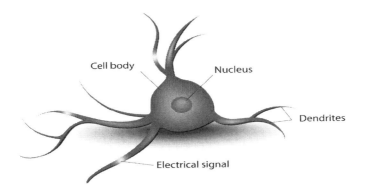

Mind Maps® appear to reflect, reinforce and encourage our natural thinking patterns.

PIXEL OR HAND?

Excellent mind mapping programs exist that make mind mapping easier and quicker than doing it manually. But the Mind Map® purists would probably put a contract out on me for saying this. And they might have a point.

Mind Maps® work best when they're a personal representation of your thoughts and ideas; that's what makes them unique. The best way of representing the inner workings of your mind is to use your own fair hand, not some pre-designed, prescriptive computer graphical user interface.

And that claim is backed up by the science behind the brain/hand link.

Neuroscience has proven that more neurons (brain cells) are connected to our hands than any other part of the body. So creating Mind Maps® manually engages more of the brain than being tethered to a computer screen. Childish pictures on our

Mind Map® (see above!) may be a small price to pay for greater mental engagement.

HOW DO MIND MAPS® HELP US? A SUMMARY

- They keep us engaged in the planning process, because they're fun to create

- They're memorable, because they're unique and personal to us

- They capture a lot of information on one page, giving us an overview of the entire document or subject

- They allow us to see connections between disparate elements of the topic that we might not see in traditional linear notes

- They can help structure a document

- By using words, images, shapes, symbols, colours, codes, dimensions, associations, lists and numbers, they engage and stimulate our whole brain

- They help clarify, develop and refine our message

'PAGE FRIGHT' BE GONE!

Mind Maps® offer another vital benefit, too. If you suffer from writer's block or 'page fright' — where the blank page or screen sends you running for the hills — then think about using a mindmapping program to create your document.

Not only can you plan and structure your document as described above, but you can also use it to draft your text. In any mind mapping software, simply type your text into the Notes section of each topic or branch. As the Mind Map® is radiant and not linear, it doesn't matter where you start; you can start drafting anywhere. That freedom will liberate you from the mindset that says you must draft sequentially.

Finally, geniuses like Charles Darwin and Leonardo da Vinci instinctively used proto-Mind Maps®. Here's Darwin's sketch of the tree of evolution in his 1837 notebook, which appears to follow the natural architecture of a Mind Map®:

FOOD FOR THOUGHT

If you're not already a Mind Map® convert, check it out. Look at Tony and Barry Buzan's excellent *The Mind Map Book* (BBC, 2010), or the website http://imindmap.com. Then buy a Mind Map® program or get a large sheet of white paper or card and some coloured crayons, pens or markers, and have a go. Revert to childhood for a while.

Find what works for you. Having banged on about Mind Maps® for the last few pages, I recognise they're not for everyone. An alternative is to use Post-it notes: simply write ideas as they come to you — one idea per note — and stick them on a wall or large piece of paper. Then play around with them and re-arrange them in a way that makes sense to you. Whatever method you use, your goal is to get clear about your topic, sub-topics and the connections between them.

The bottom line: in my humble opinion, planning is the most creative — and the most cerebral — part of the writing process. So the more fun and engaging you can make it, the likelier you are to do it. Map out your thoughts and ideas to clarify your understanding of the topic and your message to the reader... till your Clarity Bell rings.

rhetorica® Technique #4:

Establish Your Objective

If Technique #3 is about nailing your message to the reader, then this is about clarifying how you want your reader's behaviour to change when they get that message.

It's about defining the objective, purpose or goal of your communication.

> I use **F.F.A.** — **Facts. Feelings. Actions.**
>
> Let's look at each letter, but in the order of Facts and Actions, then Feelings.

WHAT <u>F</u>ACTS DO YOU WANT YOUR READER TO KNOW?

What you want your reader to *know* will vary enormously, depending on what you're writing and who your reader is.

If you're writing a bid, tender or proposal for instance, there will be many things you want them to know, e.g. your understanding of their needs; your proposed solution, approach, team and price; the great benefits they'll get when they appoint you; your track record with similar organisations or contracts.

If you're writing a letter to a neighbour about a party wall dispute, you might want them to know that you've got legal insurance, so you're not scared to go to court. If you're a student and you're writing your Personal Statement for a university application, you'd want the admissions tutor to know why you wanted to study that particular course or degree and what internships or work experience you'd done to demonstrate that interest.

The challenge with facts is knowing your reader well enough to judge which ones they need and which ones they don't. In other words, pitching at the right level of information and detail. Too little detail and they'll feel frustrated; too much and they'll be overwhelmed or bored.

A Mind Map® can help you see the range of your knowledge of a topic. Your job — knowing the reader as you do — is to select what's critical to them and omit the rest.

WHAT ACTION DO YOU WANT YOUR READER TO TAKE?

What do you want them to actually do as a result of reading your words?

The list is endless. You might want them to respond to your letter of complaint and refund your money, agree to meet you to discuss a business proposal, add your company to their preferred supplier list, renew their subscription, or drop their legal action against you.

Persuasive writing is not about impressing your reader with fancy words, building fluid sentences with lovely cadences or parading your grammatical prowess. It's about using the written word to change your reader's behaviour in an observable way. Technique #17, Get Your Reader To Take Action, goes to town on this.

WHAT DO YOU WANT YOUR READER TO FEEL?

Where facts and action are relatively straightforward, feelings are often overlooked, especially in business writing. That may be because they're more challenging, or because people think that emotion has no place in business. But we neglect it at our peril.

Think about a recent or live document and list all the emotions you might want your reader to feel when they're reading or have read your document. I'll go and make a cup of tea while you're doing that...

[Noises off: sound of water pouring into a kettle, kettle being switched on, boiling, water being poured into a cup, then the silent brew...]

... How did you get on?

Here's my list, in no particular order:

- Confidence / trust

- Desire

- Inspiration

- Anger, outrage

- Excitement / enthusiasm

- Motivation

- Patriotism

- Fear

- Greed

- Relief/reassurance/comfort

- Self-value, self-esteem

Confidence and **trust** in your product, service or advice are vital, especially if you're asking your reader to part with money. People are unlikely to invest in you, emotionally or financially, if they don't trust you. How do you engender this positive emotion? Through *evidence*. Demonstrate a successful track record and 'credentialise' yourself with client references, case studies and testimonials. Showing how others have benefited from trusting you reassures the reader and makes them feel it's less risky to do what you're asking them to do. See Technique #8, Convince Your Reader With Evidence, for more on this.

Desire is about making your reader *want* what you're writing about. Arouse it by reinforcing the benefits to them of what you're proposing. Or tell a story (Technique #9) that they can relate to, so they place themselves in the action and see themselves enjoying those benefits. Good case studies do this.

Inspiration results from enlisting the reader's higher values, e.g. justice, courage, self-sacrifice and charity, as a passport to associated self-esteem. Voluntary organisations often use this tactic in their fund-raising communications, appealing to the reader's nobler values to make a difference or be a force for good in the world.

As writers, we can use the energy of **anger/outrage** to change the reader's behaviour. Make them angry by shining the light on a barbaric practice or unjust situation in the world, then channel that energy into donating time or money to correct it. Charities and voluntary organisations do this a lot in their marketing literature.

Excitement and **enthusiasm** are hugely important emotions in persuasion, especially in business, where most writing is dull. This is because most business writers talk more about themselves than the reader (an instant turn-off), and they fail to make the benefits compelling. Excite your reader by telling them what they're going to *get* when they buy your product or follow your advice, rather than what you're going to *do*. 'Get' is a powerful weapon in our persuasive arsenal.

Similar to excitement, **motivation** comes from answering the reader's primordial question, 'WIIFM?' ('What's In It For Me?'). To borrow from NLP again, if their motivational make-up is more 'towards', they'll tend to be attracted to the idea of getting something valuable and/or desirable if they do as you suggest. If, however, their motivation is 'away from', then they'll be more motivated by the idea of avoiding something risky or undesirable.

Patriotism can be a powerful way of affecting the reader, too. Reminding them what's great about their country and urging them to preserve it is a positive motivation. A more coercive approach would be to remind them of their duty to their country of origin, as the flip-side to their civic rights, creating a feeling of guilt and obligation to move them to do what you want.

Fear — and its cousins anxiety, worry, concern — is a giant lever in our persuasion machine. We can scare people into action by reminding them what they stand to lose by not doing what we want them to do, e.g. their job, promotion, power, control, profit, advantage, reputation, control or influence. They might worry about making a mistake, taking the wrong decision, hiring the wrong person, failing in some way. The list is endless.

We can also use scarcity as a springboard to fear. By limiting the supply or availability of something the reader sees as valuable or desirable, we create a sense of urgency in them and a fear of missing out.

Most economists recognise the impact on markets of sentiment. In a bear market, for instance, the predominant emotion is fear.

Greed is another huge lever, the flipside to fear and a bedfellow of desire. We can use it by stressing to the reader what they will *get* (that word again), how they'll profit from whatever you're urging them to do. And profit doesn't have to mean money; it could mean influence, control, power, status, image or reputation — in fact, much of what they're scared of losing. In a bull market, the predominant emotion is greed.

Relief/reassurance/comfort comes from convincing the reader that they've finally found someone who can answer their questions or give them the critical information they seek. A lawyer once told me that a key piece of information about competition law had stopped a client of his going to prison.

Self-value, self-esteem: writing which is personalised to the reader's particular needs and agenda will make them feel special and valued. This is a subtler form of flattery than merely praising the reader's skills, attributes or achievements.

So, what's the role of feeling and emotion in persuasion?

It's all thanks to this guy...

... the grandfather of rhetoric, a pupil of Plato and tutor to Alexander the Great. None other than Aristotle.

Aristotle identified the three elements of persuasion that are as relevant to us in the 21st century as they were in the fourth century BC:

Ethos: the character, reputation or credibility of the 'persuader', i.e. you, the writer.

Logos: ancient Greek for word, this is about appealing to the reader's sense of logic and reason.

Pathos: ancient Greek for passion or emotion. Aristotle believed this was the king of the three. The reason why Feelings in F.F.A. are so important is this: logic makes people think, but emotion makes them *act*.

'BUT ISN'T THIS JUST MANIPULATION?'

No. What distinguishes manipulation from persuasion is that the former is sneaky, underhand and only benefits the writer, while the latter either benefits both parties (i.e. a 'win/win') or just the reader.

HOW TO USE F.F.A. IN YOUR PLANNING: A NON-BUSINESS EXAMPLE

A family friend called Debbie, a single mum with a young son, who had lived in the same area of London as us for 25 years, learnt that the municipal council was planning to re-house her in a distant part of the borough. This would have taken her away from her local support network of friends and carers, making it hard for her to work late and look after her three-year-old son, probably forcing her to leave her job and go on benefits. She appealed to her local Member of Parliament (MP) for his help.

Although her well written email succeeded — the Housing Department eventually let her stay in the local area — she could have made the email even easier and quicker by creating this F.F.A. table (remember, this is for Debbie to define what she wanted the MP to know, feel and do):

FACTS	FEELINGS	ACTION
What she wants the reader to know	What she wants the reader to feel	What she wants the reader to do
Single mum with 3-yr-old son working full-time as NHS Administrator on £16,000 p.a.	Sympathetic (to her situation)	Lean on the Council to re-house Debbie in the local area
Made homeless due to family breakdown	Concerned, anxious (about the impact on Debbie and her son, and losing her taxes and contribution to the local economy)	
Wandsworth Council tenant since 2/12		
May be moved to distant part of borough away from my support network		
Stressed: I might have to leave my job due to the added transport and child care costs and have to rely on state help	Motivated to help	
Want to stay where I am, close to support network of friends and carers that my son is used to		

The tapering pattern of text in this table is a classic shape: we tend to have lots of information to convey in the Facts column, what we want our reader to feel usually congregates around a handful of emotions and the action we want them to take is often expressed in one line. Yours doesn't have to be like that, but that's a pattern I've recognised over the years.

Here's the email Debbie could have written to her MP, as a result of defining her F.F.A.:

Subject: Debbie N — *Request to be re-housed in Balham*

Dear Mr [name of Member of Parliament],

I am a 27-year-old single mother with a three-year-old son, working full-time as an NHS Administrator at the Evelina Children's Hospital, Westminster, on £16,000 a year. We have been Wandsworth Council tenants since February 2012, when we became homeless due to a family breakdown; we are currently in temporary accommodation in Nightingale Square, Balham. I have lived in this area all my life.

I understand from my Wandsworth Council caseworker, Cheryl P, that I might be re-housed in Battersea or Roehampton, where there is a lot of housing stock. My concern is being moved away from my local support network of friends and carers and the impact this will have on the quality of life of my son and I.

My job often requires me to work late, e.g. in Casualty, and I rely heavily on my local network of close friends and godparents to collect him from after-school club and look after him until I get home. Only last week, for instance, I worked till 11pm on three separate occasions, collecting my son shortly before midnight. And when he is unwell and can't go to school, I am even more reliant on these people to look after him the whole day and sometimes the evening, too.

My son currently attends Balham Nursery School and Children's Centre and is due to be going there full-time from September 2012.

He is settled at the school and all his friends live locally. Our support network lives on the following Balham roads: Ravenslea, Endlesham, Gosberton, Emmanuel, Thornton.

Moving us out of the area would force me to pay somebody to collect my son from Balham and travel home on public transport, often late at night. These are costs I cannot afford: I would have to give up work and live on benefits, which I don't want to do. I have voiced my concerns to my caseworker, but she cannot guarantee that I will stay in Balham. The thought and the uncertainty around all this are stressing and depressing me.

My support network has enabled me to do so much. I can go to work and perform my job to a high standard. I can keep my son safe and happy. When I need a break and time to myself, I depend on them and they are always there for me. Taking them away from us will be extremely detrimental to me and my son and how we live in the future. The economy will also be losing a tax-payer and gaining a single mother who, rather than relying on a support network, will be relying on the state.

I am happy to stay in temporary housing until something comes up in Balham. But I am asking whether you could please use your influence with the Council to see that this can happen.

With kind regards and thanks
Debbie N

HOW TO USE F.F.A. IN YOUR PLANNING:
A BUSINESS EXAMPLE

Imagine this scenario: you've been tasked with inviting a high profile executive in your industry to be the keynote speaker at your annual sales conference. Create a three-column table with the three headings and fill it in, like this:

FACTS	FEELINGS	ACTION
I want the reader to know that…	I want the reader to feel…	I want the reader to…
We'd like her to be the keynote speaker at our annual sales conference in Switzerland next August.	Flattered Valued, special Anxious (a competitor may get asked if she dithers)	Agree to be the keynote speaker at our sales conference
She tops our list of candidates: our CEO heard her speak last year at the Sales Executive Council and insisted we book her.		
If she is not available, we have other high profile candidates in reserve.	Excited, enthusiastic Motivated, greedy Reassured	
She will address top industry leaders, then enjoy a private lunch with them afterwards.		
She will get a generous speaking fee and her company will get much media attention.		
We will take care of all the logistics, including her accommodation and return flight from New York.		

The F.F.A. table acts as a checklist for all the points you want to cover when you're drafting. The more thinking you put into it and the more detailed your table, the easier and quicker your drafting will be. I'd go even further and say this: when you do F.F.A. thoroughly, you break the back of your document before you even start drafting.

FOOD FOR THOUGHT

1. Pick a document to test this technique on: it might be a live, recent or soon-to-be-tackled piece of communication.

2. Type or write F, F and A in a three-column table at the top of your document.

3. Now populate each letter in as much detail as possible.

4. Use the table as an aide-memoire while you're drafting.

The bottom line: F.F.A. forces you to think about your reader and the three dimensions of their behaviour that you want to affect. Using the acronym properly (as in the three-column table) helps you to nail your purpose and makes drafting easier. Think of it as your magnetic north to guide you as you draft.

Although I've presented Techniques #3 and #4 consecutively, in practice I often mind map the topic and define my objective at the same time. Sometimes facts, feelings and action form three branches of my Mind Map®. This helps me to see which aspects of the topic and/or the communication will best deliver my objective.

Remember: facts may make people think, but *feelings* make them *act*.

rhetorica® Technique #5:

Structure For Maximum Impact

Structure is more important than language.

Why do I say that?

No matter how well you write, if your content isn't arranged in a clear, logical sequence that the reader can easily follow, if they can't discern a clear structure, they're likely to give up. Disaster.

So, how do you nail 'structure'?

Much of your thinking so far in planning mode has been divergent, especially if you've done a Mind Map® of your document or topic. You've generated ideas, thoughts, insights and options. Your thinking has been broad and radiant.

Now that it's time to structure your communication — the final step in the planning process — it's also time for your thinking to change. Choosing a structure or running order for your document involves cutting some of those options in favour of others; you can't (and mustn't) include every idea you've come up with. So, as you move from brainstorming to selecting, your thinking must narrow. It must move from divergent to convergent.

This shift in focus is not only important for our structure. It also primes our brain for drafting, where we will be sifting, sorting and selecting words to express ourselves clearly and precisely. The skill of drafting – as we will see in Section II – involves thinking that is more like a laser than a light bulb.

WHY MOST WRITING STRUCTURES FAIL

Most pieces of communication I come across are structured like this:

Exhibit A

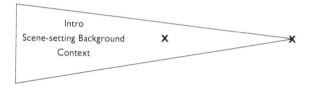

Reading left to right, they spend the first pages or slides introducing the topic and background, or talking about themselves and/or their organisation. They may call it 'Introduction', 'Scene-Setting', 'Exposition' or 'Context'; I call it guff.

The author mistakenly believes that this is of interest to the reader and will convince them to read on. Trouble is, you're delaying what the reader is most interested in — the benefits to them of doing whatever it is you want them to do (remember, they're more interested in themselves than in you). You're relegating your main message to the end of the document in the climax of your argument (second X) or burying it somewhere in the middle (first X).

This approach to organising your ideas is known as deductive logic, i.e. it leads the reader step-by-step through a linear argument or evidence to the conclusion or main message. It gives the evidence first, then the message.

There are three risks in this approach:

- the reader loses interest and stops reading before they reach your main message

- the reader loses patience if you put too many ideas in the sequence

- the argument may fall over if the reader disagrees with any step in the sequence

Just because you analysed the problem or the issue *deductively*, don't assume that that's how your reader wants it presented.

Instead, invert your structural pyramid to look like this:

Exhibit B

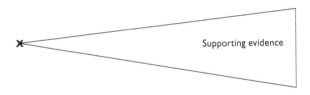

Hit the reader as soon as you reasonably can with your main message – that may be the chief benefit of appointing your firm, your major recommendation, a key finding from a study or the main point of your letter. If in doubt, answer the age-old question, 'What's in it for me?' ('WIIFM?'). Put the stuff about you later in the document once you've grabbed and held the reader's attention with what they are most interested in.

This approach to organising your ideas is known as inductive logic, i.e. it gives the main message first, followed by the evidence, creating pyramids of ideas. This brings three benefits:

- you engage the reader because they get what they're most interested in *first*

- they save time by getting the answer early, with the option of reviewing the evidence if/when they want to

- your argument doesn't fall down if they disagree with one of the supporting ideas

This is what newspapers do so well. They summarise the story in the first paragraph: that's the only thing you need to read to decide whether to continue reading or move on.

There's a cliché that every document must have a beginning, a middle and an end. What we're doing here is starting with the end.

WHY MOST PEOPLE DON'T START WITH THE END

The deductive approach to communication (evidence, then message) is a throwback to how we were taught at school.

When you did an experiment in science class, you were probably told to follow a sequence like: Hypothesis – Risk Assessment – Method – Results – Conclusion – Evaluation. And when you had to write an essay, the sequence was something like: Introduction – Point – Evidence – Analysis – Conclusion.

We crunch the numbers, do the research, speak to experts, analyse the findings, *then* pen the conclusion. The conclusion is at the end because that's when we write it; it's logical to put it there. By definition, conclusions (from the Latin *concludere*, to shut, close, end, decide, resolve, determine or settle) tend to sit either right at the end or near it.

'That's fine at school', as Jon Moon says in *How to make an impact* (FT Prentice Hall, 2008), 'because the teacher already knows the answer and just wants to see how close you get to it. But in business [and other fields where communication is key], our reader only knows the answer when we tell them. And they'd rather hear it sooner than later, so they have context to judge the detail that follows'.

It's counter-intuitive to put our conclusion at the front — to start with the end — because that doesn't reflect our own logical journey. But it's much more helpful to the reader.

HOW DO WE NAIL THE STRUCTURE OF OUR COMMUNICATION?

If you've done a Mind Map® (see Technique #3), a 'quick win' is to number the main branches (coined by Tony Buzan as 'Basic Ordering Ideas' or BOIs) connected to the central image in the order that will make most sense to the reader. That numbered sequence then represents the structure or running order of our communication.

Another approach is to use Post-it notes, which I mentioned in Technique #3.

Write in big, bold letters the title of all the sections of your communication, each on its own Post-it. Then place them on a wall or whiteboard to represent your running order. That way you can assess at a glance the skeleton of your document. The obvious advantage is that the Post-its are not fixed: you can move them and play around with the structure to see what makes most sense.

And you can do the same for each section of the document. Capture the main ideas or pieces of information on their own Post-its and re-order them on the wall until you're happy with the running order.

What I like about using Post-its is that you're on your feet and applying that powerful brain/hand connection I mentioned in the context of Mind Maps® in Technique #3. I'm a fan of making planning as tactile and as physical as possible.

STRUCTURAL DEVICES TO HELP US

If language is about choice, structure is about navigation. It's about making it easy for your reader to see the shape or gist of the document and find the bits they want to read and the bits they'd rather skip. It saves them time and effort. If, on the other hand, you make it hard for them to find what they want and they give up, then all your wonderful prose is for nought.

So far we've talked about an important structural principle that delivers clarity and impact: start with the end.

Now let's talk about two practical *devices* that aid reader navigation, especially for printed matter: a contents list and subheadings.

STRUCTURAL DEVICE 1: TABLE OF CONTENTS

If you're writing a longish document, like a report or a brochure, then a table of contents is essential. It's satnav for your document: it makes it easy for the reader to find what they want.

When reviewing a document, I always look at the table of contents first. It's like looking at an X-ray of the document: it helps me to see both the underlying structure of the document and the author's mindset. What do I mean by that? Here's an example, from a law firm's bid document:

Contents

No prizes for guessing the mindset of the author. The predominant word in this list of contents is 'our'. The writer is more interested in themselves and their own organisation than in the client. They're being author-centric, not reader-centric. What would be better words than *our*? The magic words *you* and *your* (Technique #1).

If you do add a list of contents, it must have page numbers and they must be accurate. There's nothing more galling than expecting to find a chapter or section on a particular page, only to land in the middle rather than at the beginning of that section. Pagination is such an easy thing to check that to screw it up screams world-class incompetence.

STRUCTURAL DEVICE 2: SUBHEADINGS

While contents lists give an overview of a whole document, subheadings (also known as 'sub-sections' or 'cross-heads'), like the one directly above, help us navigate *within* it.

When it comes to longer documents, most people don't slavishly read from the very first word to the last, do they? (Do you?) They scan the subheadings to get the gist of the story and decide which bits to read and which to skip, saving them valuable time and energy. Subheadings are like stepping-stones that allow the reader to hop, skip and jump through the document. And like any form of signposting, the more specific, descriptive and informative they are, the better.

So, let's see how this all works in practice — arranging material logically, starting with the end and using subheadings.

Here are three different versions (A, B, C) of an assessment of a school, each progressively improving on the previous (except, of course, for A!). Each version gets a grade at the end.

VERSION A

Assessment of XYZ School: findings

- Literacy is a strength of the school. It is promoted not only in English, but across all subjects.

- The quality of teaching leads to exceptionally good outcomes for students, especially at GCSE.

- The hardware in the ICT suite needs replacing, and four of the classroom electronic whiteboards are not working.

- Lessons are characterised by high expectations, strong teacher subject knowledge, skilful questioning and stimulating activities — particularly in English, maths and history.

- In 2014 achievement at GCSE was well above the national average, with 86% of students gaining five or more GCSEs at A* to C grades, including English and maths.

- There is a budget deficit. The school has had to sell its sports ground and shares playing fields with another school 45 minutes away. This is increasing transport costs and reducing student participation in sports.

- Disabled students and those with special educational needs make good progress, because teaching assistants are motivated and well trained.

- Literacy levels are high. Students can articulate ideas and opinions with confidence. They enjoy reading and use the school library, set texts and their own reading material extensively, across both fiction and non-fiction.

- In 2014, the number of A-level passes at grades A* to B was below the national average.

- AS-level results for 2014 were also below the national average, with only 39% of students achieving grades A to B.

- The gym is in need of refurbishment / modernisation: dry rot was found in the roof timbers and the equipment is old.

Version A grade: FAIL. This is an unstructured, unordered shopping list/brain dump of findings that says to the reader: 'Here's what I found. You work it out.' This is rude, unhelpful, lazy writing.

VERSION B

Assessment of XYZ School

Conclusion: the budget deficit needs to be cut and Sixth Form performance improved, but overall the school is doing well, especially at GCSE

STRENGTHS

- Lessons are characterised by high expectations, strong teacher subject knowledge, skilful questioning and stimulating activities — particularly in English, maths and history.

- The quality of teaching leads to exceptionally good outcomes for students, especially at GCSE.

- In 2014 achievement at GCSE was well above the national average, with 86% of students gaining five or more GCSEs at A* to C grades, including English and maths.

- Literacy is a strength of the school. It is promoted not only in English, but across all subjects. Students can articulate ideas and opinions with confidence. They enjoy reading and use the school library, set texts and their own reading material extensively, across both fiction and non-fiction.

- Disabled students and those with special educational needs make good progress, because the teaching assistants are motivated and well trained.

WEAKNESSES

- In 2014, the number of A-level passes at grades A* to B was below the national average.

- There is a budget deficit. The school has had to sell its sports ground and shares playing fields with another school 45 minutes away. This is increasing transport costs and reducing student participation in sports.

- AS-level results for 2014 were also below the national average, with only 39% of students achieving grades A to B.

- The gym is in need of refurbishment/modernisation: dry rot was found in the roof timbers and the equipment is old.

- The hardware in the ICT suite needs replacing, and four of the classroom electronic whiteboards are not working.

Version B grade: B+. Putting the conclusion (the 'end') at the top and sorting the findings into strengths and weaknesses make it easier for the reader to understand the assessment. However, this version is still an un-scannable bulleted list, due to the lack of subheadings under the umbrella headings of 'Strengths' and 'Weaknesses' and the haphazard order of the findings.

VERSION C

Assessment of XYZ School

Conclusion: the budget deficit needs to be cut and Sixth Form performance improved, but overall the school is doing well, especially at GCSE

Strengths

Exceptional teaching and student outcomes	The quality of teaching leads to exceptionally good outcomes for students, especially at GCSE. Lessons are characterised by high expectations, strong teacher subject knowledge, skilful questioning and stimulating activities — particularly in English, maths and history.
Literacy is promoted	Literacy is a strength of the school. It is promoted not only in English, but across all subjects. Students can articulate ideas and opinions with confidence. They enjoy reading and use the school library, set texts and their own reading material extensively, across both fiction and non-fiction.
2014 GCSEs above national average	In 2014 achievement at GCSE was well above the national average, with 86% of students gaining five or more GCSEs at A* to C grades, including English and maths.
Provision for disabled/SEN students	Disabled students and those with special educational needs make good progress, because teaching assistants are motivated and well trained.

Weaknesses

2014 A-levels below national average	In 2014, the number of A-level passes at grades A* to B was below the national average. AS-level results for 2014 were also below the national average, with only 39% of students achieving grades A to B.
Facilities are run-down	There is a budget deficit. The school has had to sell its sports ground and must share playing fields with another school 45 minutes away. This is increasing transport costs and reducing student participation in sports. The gym is also in need of refurbishment and modernisation: dry rot was found in the roof timbers and the equipment is old. The hardware in the ICT suite needs replacing, and four of the classroom electronic whiteboards are not working.

Version C grade: A*. We've turned the bulleted list into a two-column table, applying Jon Moon's WiT (Word in Tables) system[2]. We've made the text easier to read by putting it in narrower, newspaper-style columns. Under the umbrella headings of 'Strengths' and 'Weaknesses', we've grouped the findings that belong together and put them in descending order of magnitude. In the left-hand column we've created subheadings for each strength or weakness which summarise the conclusion

---

2 This section is modelled on and inspired by Jon Moon's excellent book, *How to make an impact*, FT Prentice Hall, and his signature WiT system.

(the 'end'), and we've given them more prominence by emboldening them.

The result is a piece of communication that is scannable, readable and visually interesting.

That's the power of structure.

FOOD FOR THOUGHT

1. Identify your main message — the one thing you want your reader to take away from your communication. That may be your conclusion, main finding, major insight, chief recommendation, top benefit.

2. Put that at the top; lead with that.

3. Congratulations! In one fell swoop, you've transformed the structure and impact of your document.

The bottom line: structure is more important than language, as it's the delivery mechanism for your message and objective. If your communication is ill-structured, the message is lost and the objective missed; your communication collapses. You wouldn't install up-market cladding and expensive sash windows in the exterior of a building that was structurally unsound, would you?

THE BOTTOM LINE FOR SECTION I, PLANNING:

If you want to write more clearly and with greater impact, you must plan. Use the acronym S-T-O-R-M (Structure – Timing – Objective – Reader – Message) to nail the five elements of planning.

S-T-O-R-M is merely a reminder of the five elements; it's not the order we do them in. Setting time aside to plan should be the very first thing you do, and your reader should be constantly in your thoughts. Other than that, S, O and M overlap and can often be done simultaneously. For example, you can define the high-level structure, objective and message of your communication in one Mind Map®.

When we use drafting to clarify our thoughts we cage our creativity, because language is better at capturing ideas than creating them. But by making planning a deliberate, purposeful activity, we separate thinking from writing. This allows us to think more clearly, more expansively, more divergently.

> ## *Most plans are useless, but the act of planning is indispensable.*
>
> Napoleon Bonaparte (allegedly)

Now you've planned, it's time to move from thought, analysis, imagination, research and structure… to language, word-choice and Section II, Drafting.

SECTION II:
Drafting

If language is not correct, then what is said is not what is meant; if what is said is not what is meant, then what ought to be done remains undone.

Confucius

rhetorica® Technique #6:

Grab Your Reader's Attention

Attention is the first thing to get from your reader. And there are a number of ways to get it.

If you're writing an email, it will be your subject line:

Subject: Failed order 203-3265851 — pls refund my money

If you're writing a letter, it will be your opening line or topic reference:

Re: Poor service at your restaurant, 12 March

If you're writing a blog or article, it may be a combo of image + headline:

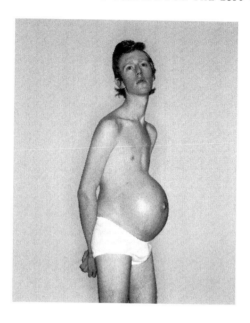

WHY NOT?

The headline (not the 'title', as some people call it) is the most common device for stopping the reader in their tracks and getting them to read, click, like, share or pin the article beneath.

But how do you write powerful attention-grabbers?

A bit like F.F.A. when setting your purpose or objective (Technique #4), it helps to answer these three simple questions when considering your headline:

1. What job must the headline do?

2. What, if anything, do I want the reader to feel?

3. Which headline techniques lend themselves best to 1 and 2?

Get clear about the role of your headline: do you want it to inform, interest or move your reader? Here's what I mean.

You might need to send an all-staff email warning people that, due to a server outage, there'll be no email next Friday. You don't need people to feel anything (although they may well feel relief at the news); you're merely conveying practical information, so the subject line,

> *No email Friday 18 Sept*

... would probably do (adding the date lets staff who were or will be away that Friday know they can safely ignore the message).

On the other hand, you might want your headline to spark your reader's interest — and hint that the content is intellectually meaty and technical:

> *What caused the credit crunch?*

> *Statistical analysis of wage distribution — why the latest model is flawed*

> *Court of Appeal: prior settlement bars patent validity challenge*

The third job you might want your headline to do is to move your reader. Again, this echoes what we discussed in Technique #4, Establish Your Objective: what do you want your reader to feel, to get them to read your article or blog? Fear, greed, lust, outrage, defiance, shock, awe, revulsion, curiosity... the list is endless. The point is to engage them by eliciting an emotional reaction.

For many, the *'Je suis Charlie'* campaign (in memory of the 12 journalists of the French satirical newspaper *Charlie Hebdo* murdered in January 2015) evokes feelings of solidarity, outrage and defiance of violent extremism.

Alternatively, you might want your headline to shock or provoke. Here's one from the clothing retailer Timberland:

WE STOLE THEIR LAND, THEIR BUFFALO AND THEIR WOMEN.

THEN WE WENT BACK FOR THEIR SHOES.

I've identified 13 techniques, listed below, for creating attention-grabbing headlines. They're not mutually exclusive: you can combine a number of them in your headline.

1. THE TWIST / SURPRISE

Also known as the 'pattern-breaker', this style of headline pulls the rug from under the reader by leading them down one thought path, only to abruptly change direction at the end. *The Economist* print ads are legendary at this:

> *"I never read* The Economist.*"*
> *Management trainee. Aged 42.*

> *In opinion polls, 100% of* Economist *readers had one*

> *"Economist readers welcome."*
> *Sperm donor clinic*

Sometimes the Twist is just a new take on an old topic:

CANCER CURES SMOKING
(Cancer Patients Aid Association)

2. THE JUXTAPOSITION (OR CONTRASTING PAIRS)

Probing the cause of diabetes, one pizza at a time

Cash if you die, cash if you don't
(life insurance product)

Get a degree without going to uni
(Open University)

Live working or die fighting: how the working class went global

Putin dares, Obama dithers
(note the alliteration of the 'd' sound)

3. THE WORD PLAY (OR DOUBLE MEANING)

Wake up to the importance of sleep

Ever heard people talking about their Volkswagens? They go on and on and on

Don't get left out: download your new entry PIN here

Old age: a thing of the past?

Sparks & Mensa
(The Economist)

Great minds like a think
(The Economist)

Think someone under the table
(The Economist)

4. THE HEADLINE/STANDFIRST COMBO

More and more professional services firms writing technical blogs or client alerts about industry developments are using this. The idea is simple: grab the reader's attention with a dramatic headline, then give an explanatory one-liner (known as the 'standfirst') right underneath it:

HMRC is closing in
New tax laws are making it harder to set up
offshore tax havens

It's a class act
New UK class action procedures come into force
1 October

Leaders in driverless cars
What happens when left-wing politicians
confront new technologies

5A. THE QUESTION

A tried and trusted technique, this. A relevant, interesting question engages the reader because it piques their curiosity or sparks a mental image. The human brain craves completion, so the merest hint of an information gap or lack of knowledge makes the reader want to know more.

What really caused the credit crunch?
(note the alliteration of the 'cr' sound)

Why is the divorce rate soaring?

Where have the dotcom profits gone?

How real is climate change?

FCO Healthcare: is it fit for the 21ˢᵗ century?

5B. THE QUESTION + THE MAGIC WORD(S)

The magic words *you* and *your* make the reader feel as if you're talking to them and them alone. Combining these with a question that addresses the reader on a topic that resonates with them will engage them:

You're an adult now. But are you still afraid of the dark?

New UK class action regime: what do you need to know?

Do you really need to keep 40 plastic bags at home?

Do you close the bathroom door even when you're the only one home?

Are you a scruncher or a folder?
(Andrex loo paper — there's a pattern emerging here)

6. THE COMMAND OR INSTRUCTION

You're telling the reader what to do, by using a verb in the 'imperative mood'.

Click *here to register for the course*

Apply now for your early-bird discount

Find out more about a career in teaching

Fix your high staff turnover

7. THE KILLER FACT

'Killer Facts' are memorable stats or statements that cut through the detail and stun the reader into action. Journalists and politicians pick them up as sound bites. They're known as 'killers' because they kill off opponents' arguments quicker than a worthy study or well-researched report[3].

Two works of man are visible from space: the Great Wall of China and the fires raging in the rainforest

Bananas are subject to more EC regulations than AK47s

Armed conflict costs Africa $18 billion a year

A child dies every four seconds from preventable causes

There are two bullets for every person on the planet

8. THE NUMBER

Quantifying a fact implies authority, precision and complete-ness, and reassures the reader that you know what you're talking about. And received wisdom suggests that odd numbers are more memorable than even ones. So if you're listing bene-fits in a bid document, say, try — as naturally as you can — to sort them into an odd number.

---

3   Oxfam GB Research Guidelines November 2012

Whistle-blower disclosures up 17%

37 tips for getting your blog read

7 simple six-pack exercises

17 ways to generate more leads

New bug threatens more than 200,000 sites

*Seven-and-a-half principles for winning
more bids and tenders*
(the strapline of my first book, *Winner Takes All*)

Notice how many of the headlines above included seven?

Seven — and numbers with seven in them — is powerful. In 2014 mathematician Alex Bellos conducted an online poll of 30,000 people, who voted seven their most popular number (three and eight were runners-up). Bellos claims it's because seven is the only number among those we can count on our hands that can't be multiplied or divided within that group of numbers. One to five can be doubled and still stay within the group; six, eight and ten can be halved; nine can be divided by three. But seven is a Loner; the Outsider, as Bellos calls it. It's a prime number that cannot neatly be divided by anything other than itself and one.

There are seven days of the week, seven colours of the rainbow, seven notes on a musical scale, seven seas and seven continents. Snow White ran off to live with seven dwarves, there were seven brides for seven brothers, Shakespeare described the seven ages of man, Sinbad the Sailor had seven voyages. When Ian Fleming was looking for a code for his spy hero, only 007 had the right ring. And I wonder if I chose 21 techniques for rhetorica® because 21 is a multiple of seven?

Humans are sensitive to special arithmetical patterns, so associating seven with a group of things makes them special, too.

Quick tip on numbers: whether to spell out numbers or use figures (also called 'numerals') is largely a matter of writers' preference, i.e. it's more a stylistic convention than a hard and fast rule. The two most influential US guidebooks for publishers, editors and writers are the *Associated Press Stylebook* and *the Chicago Manual of Style*. Here in the UK I defer to *The Economist Style Guide*. Professional writers and editors also use *The Guardian and Observer Style Guide* and Oxford University Press's *Hart's Rules*.

This states that numbers one to ten we spell out (as here); 11 and above we write as digits, e.g. 27, 103, 365. The exceptions to this rule are units of measurement (4 metres, 7m^3, 9 miles), page numbers, dates (5th July), times (06:30) and rhetorical figures (*death by a thousand cuts, a hundred years of solitude*).

Whichever stylebook you adhere to, be consistent.

9. THE POWER WORD

Power words are violent, visual, visceral, plain English words that have an emotional impact on the reader:

*Google **kills** Google reader*

*Public sector budgets **slashed***

*So many lives **wrecked** by booze*

*Big data is **dead**. What's next?*

10. THE NEGATIVE

Although received wisdom is that embedding a benefit in a headline works well, a 2013 study of 100 blogs ('The Dark

Science of Naming your Post', Iris Shoor) shows that negative words like *no*, *without* or *stop* generate more shares and likes than their positive counterparts:

5 things you should stop doing to be happy

The fitness app you can't live without

Apple is not the most valuable company in history

Cloud adoption: it's not about the price, stupid

11. THE METAPHOR

This is about borrowing an image or idea from one area of life to describe another:

*Kids are digging their own graves with
a knife and fork*

Inbox flooded with spam?

*The job market's a circus: are you the dancing bear,
the lion or the clown?*

The wheels of justice turn slower than ever

12. THE NEWS

People are interested in stuff that's new or different, so words like *now*, *new* and *introducing* spark interest, especially if it's linked to a benefit:

Now they can stop you ageing

New statins lower blood pressure another 5%

Welcome to New London

Introducing the dating agency with a difference

13. THE 'HOW TO'

This simple phrase tells the reader they're about to get a practical solution to a problem or challenge that they can implement immediately:

How to run a profitable workshop

How to improve your sex life

How to train your puppy

How to make partner and still have a life

How to write a book in three months

FOOD FOR THOUGHT

Take a selection of your recent email subject lines or article headlines and ask yourself:

'Are they short and punchy?'

'Are they relevant to my reader?'

'Will they inform, interest or intrigue my reader?'

'If I saw them in my inbox or online, would they get my attention?'

If you answer 'No' to any of these questions, re-visit the 13 techniques to create headlines and subheadings that stand out.

And test. Test different headlines for the same copy online and track the open and click-through rates for each. If you're writing offline, ask the reader(s) for feedback on the headline: did it grab their attention, or would they have read the piece anyway 'cos it was from you?

The bottom line: many of the headlines I've cited here have won advertising awards for their creativity, but I don't want you to feel either intimidated or compelled to suddenly become a top copywriter. Often the simplest headlines are the best. As long as your headline grabs the reader's attention and gets them to open your email or read your blog, it's done its job. The creative awards can wait.

Now you've got your reader's attention, you have to keep it. Turn over to find out how.

rhetorica® Technique #7:

Turn Features Into Benefits

In Technique #1, Write For Your Reader, we established the importance of focusing not on ourselves as the writer, but on the reader.

When we do this, everything changes.

Instead of talking about ourselves and our message, we talk about the reader's needs or goals. Instead of describing what we're going to *do*, we describe what the reader *gets* as a result. Instead of talking about the features of our product or service, we talk about the benefits to the reader.

And it's the tussle between features and benefits that I'd like to lean into here.

F.A.B.: FEATURES, ADVANTAGES, BENEFITS

F.A.B. selling is a staple of sales people around the world[4]. Yet

---

[4] The earliest reference I can find to F.A.B. is Larry Wilson's 'Sales Sonics' training course on consultative selling, developed in 1965 and delivered to the likes of Hewlett Packard, Disney and Ernst & Young.

if you're not a sales or business person, you may be hazy about the terms. So let's clarify them:

A *feature* is a characteristic, attribute or property of you or your product or service. The reader may or may not value it.

An *advantage* is what you do or your product/service does that others don't do, i.e. what differentiates it from the rest.

A *benefit* is how you, your product or your service makes someone's life better in a way that they will value; it's about the recipient getting a desirable, positive outcome. Examples of benefits include:

- A well-behaved dog

- Promotion

- Better health/fitness

- A good night's sleep

- A sizzling sex life

- Higher self-esteem

- Your dream partner/job/home

- 30% more business won

- Twice as many leads converted into sales

- Shareholder value boosted 17%

- Productivity doubled in three months

- Staff turnover cut by 42%

- Attendance raised by 9%

- Return on investment improved by 20%

(Grammar Geek note: I've expressed many of the benefits in the past participle of the verb, which we form by adding -ed to the stem of regular verbs, e.g. *boosted, converted, raised*. This emphasises the benefit as a result rather than an action.)

Trouble is, many writers confuse benefits and features, or simply list features without converting them into reader benefits. How do we make that conversion? By challenging them with 'So what?' Here's what I mean:

> *BabyGates.com was founded in 2008 and specialises in child safety products* [feature]. **So what?** *We're the market leader for child safety* [feature]. *In fact we've won more child safety awards than anybody else* [advantage]. **So what?** *We recently launched a new, deluxe, 21st century baby gate* [feature]. **So what?** *It's easy to install with special gate-style mountings and comes in a range of colours to match your home* [features]. **So what?** *It comes with a child-proof, tamper-free KiddyGuard* [feature]. **So what?** *That means your child will never push the gate over and fall down the stairs* [benefit, finally].

When it feels daft, absurd or plain negligent to ask 'So what?', chances are you've landed on the end-benefit. This simple little question forces us to drill down from the surface feature to the bedrock benefit.

Below is a list of features converted into benefits with 'So what?' Notice how there are far more words in the Benefits column than in the Features one. That's a good sign. It shows that we're going to town on the benefits to the reader, rather than just listing the features.

I'm sure you've also noticed that when we talk about features, the predominant words are *we* and *our*. Yet when we talk about benefits, the predominant words are *you* and *your*. Using these magic words shows that your mindset has shifted to being reader-centric, which is another reason to major on benefits.

The strongest benefits have three qualities: they are concrete, not abstract or woolly; specific, not generic; definite, not vague (especially if you can quantify them, as I did in the right-hand column of the bulleted list above).

Here are more fleshed out examples:

Feature	Benefit
I climbed Everest in 2013. **So *what?***	If you hire me you'll get someone who combines individual determination with a fierce team ethic. You don't reach the summit of Everest on your own. I was part of an international, inter-dependent team where everyone had distinct roles but a common goal. At 29,000 feet and −25°C, if you don't pull together as a team, you can die.
Our firm has 55,000 staff in 20 countries around the world.	You get relevant, practical and current advice on competition law from local people who know the latest regulations and, in some cases, even know the regulators.
So *what?*	What that means for you is insight into which of your new products will best satisfy the law in each particular jurisdiction and which ones carry the greatest risks in terms of anti-competitive activity.

Our journal is peer-reviewed.	You can rely on the content, currency and intellectual rigour of every academic paper in our journal. Not only has it been written by an expert in that particular field, it's been reviewed by one.
So *what?*	Authors know their work will be peer-reviewed and only published when approved by our review panel. So when you subscribe to *BioGenetics Gazette*, you know you're reading papers of the highest quality.
I love writing and won the England Young Person's Essay Writing Award. **So *what?***	That means, if you engage me, you get someone who is comfortable with writing a range of communications for your company, e.g. blog posts, magazine articles, brochures, intranet copy. You get a good first draft quickly to review, so you spend less time editing and/or re-writing the copy. The process of creating publishable material will be fast and efficient.
We only publish the results of double-blind, randomised, controlled trials (RCT) of medical products. **So *what?***	RCTs are considered the gold standard of clinical trials. That means you get the most objective test results with minimal bias that you can reliably base critical clinical and business decisions on.

Why are benefits more powerful than features?

Because benefits appeal to the reader's self-interest. Most readers are less interested in what you do and more interested in what they *get* when they appoint you, work with you or give you the job. It's OK to list the features of your product or service, provided you then relate them back to how the other person will benefit. As you may have spotted in the table above, a useful phrase for doing that is 'What that means for you is...' or 'That means you get...' then list all the benefits that will get them salivating. Alternatively, use the phrase *'What that allows you to do/get is...'*, completing the sentence with the relevant benefits.

Notice, too, how many times the magic words *you* and *your* occur in the examples above. That's a good sign.

FOOD FOR THOUGHT

Using either the blank sections in the table above or one of your own documents where you're trying to persuade someone to do something they wouldn't otherwise do, have a go at converting features into benefits with 'So what?'. This will force you to drill down to the bedrock benefits, i.e. the positive outcome for the reader.

The bottom line: three simple devices help you convert features into benefits:

1. 'So what?'

2. 'What that means for you is...'

3. 'What that allows you to do/get is...'

Benefits are more persuasive than features because they appeal to the reader's self-interest. Do that and your readers will be more open to your message.

rhetorica® Technique #8:

Convince Your Reader
With Evidence

When human beings are uncertain about a decision or course of action, they tend to look outside themselves to see what other people do. We're more likely to do something if we see other people who we think are like us doing it too.

This is known as *social proof.* And it changes behaviour.

The co-authors of *Yes! 50 secrets from the science of persuasion*[5] experimented with signs in a hotel encouraging guests to re-use their towels, rather than leave them on the bathroom floor to be washed after one use.

They created two signs that were randomly assigned to different rooms in the hotel: sign A followed the conventional style of urging guests to re-use their towels to save the environment and show respect for nature; sign B stated that the majority of guests at the hotel recycled their towels at least once during their stay (which was true).

---

5   Profile Books, 2007. N Goldstein, S Martin, R Cialdini.

When the authors analysed the data, they found that the guests who learned that most fellow guests had re-used their towels — the social proof appeal of sign B — were 26% likelier to recycle their towels than those who had sign A in their rooms.

Social proof can take many forms: references, referrals, endorsements, testimonials, industry awards, press coverage, statistics, consumer reviews and ratings, social media 'likes', 'shares' and re-tweets. All of this comes under the umbrella of *evidence*.

When we have evidence from someone other than the seller or proposer that a person, product or service is as good as they claim, we feel reassured and more confident about the choice. It makes the decision safer, less random — and easier to justify to our boss or to ourselves. As the cliché has it, 'No-one was ever fired for hiring IBM'.

REFERENCES

If you're applying for a job or bidding for a contract, the decision-maker will often ask for a reference. They seek the reassurance of speaking to someone who knows you and can vouch for your quality, either as an individual or a team.

Rather than simply leaving it up to the referee to decide what to say, however, it's important to think about the message you want your referee to give the decision-maker.

For example, if you know that the potential employer is looking for someone reliable and punctual, ask your referee to stress those points about you — provided, of course, they are true. This is about influencing someone ethically, not manipulating the truth for your own ends.

When I work with businesses on a bid or tender and they offer references from previous clients, I advise them to brief the referee to emphasise the main messages of their proposal (aka 'win-themes') when the buyer contacts them. This reinforces the buyer's perception of the bidding company and gives them further reassurance that they're making the right choice.

References (and their second-cousins, referrals) are a personal form of *endorsement*. The word comes from the Old French, *endosser*, to 'put on the back', i.e. the referee is prepared to shoulder the responsibility of speaking up for and about you to a third-party who doesn't know you.

TESTIMONIALS

Written or oral, a testimonial is a recorded reference of feedback on you or your performance, such as delegate comments on a conference, seminar or training course. From the judicial word *testimony*, to give evidence as a witness under oath, they are literally bearing witness to the quality of a person or product.

Strong testimonials have the following features:

- They are attributed to a named individual (otherwise your reader will think you've made it up)

- They rave about you, rather than being mildly positive

- They are given by someone who works in the same industry, function or type of organisation as the reader (i.e. the reader must be able to identify with them)

- They include a picture of the testimonee (video testimonials are particularly powerful)

'Rave reviews': this is no place for tepid, mealy-mouthed, 'adequate' assessments of you or your service. In fact, testimonials that sound anything less than raving could do you more harm than good.

The best testimonial I've ever had after one of my writing skills workshops was from a girl called Jude. She came up to me with her blank evaluation form and said, 'Can I write down what I *really* think of this workshop?' 'Of course', I replied, fearing the worst. As the participants said goodbye and filed out of the room, I gathered up all the evaluation forms and, you guessed it, hunted out Jude's first. In the Comments box she'd written two words:

'F*cking brilliant!'

(except she spelt out the whole word)

Now *that's* a testimonial.

Getting the reader to identify with the testimonee is important. We're more likely to do something *if we see other people who we think are like us* doing it too.

If you're applying for a university place to study applied maths and you quote a testimonial from your art teacher — no matter how raving it is — that's not going to land. The admissions tutor is likely to think, 'You don't understand me. This person's view is irrelevant to me.' Your testimonial won't carry any weight with the reader, because they can't identify with it.

Recent studies have shown that people gravitate to people, places and things that resemble themselves, based on the concept of 'favourable self-associations'. Because most people possess positive associations about themselves, they prefer things that are connected to themselves — even the letters in their own name. These self-associations influence social behaviours and major life decisions.

In 1985 Belgian researcher Jozef Nuttin showed that people like the letters in their own names more than other people like those same letters — a phenomenon he called the *name-letter effect*[6].

Psychology professors at Buffalo University, NY (Pelham, Mirenberg, Jones) built on that research with a series of studies, which proved that people are drawn to live in cities and pursue careers that resemble their names.

Their studies found that women named Florence, Georgia, Louise and Virginia were 44% likelier (above chance values) to have lived in Florida, Georgia, Louisiana and Virginia respectively.

This extended to birthday number preferences: people were disproportionately likely to live in cities whose names began with their birthday numbers (e.g., Two Harbors, Minnesota). Other studies suggested that people disproportionately choose careers which resemble their names: people called Dennis or Denise are over-represented among dentists. (The other day I watched the movie *Machine Gun Preacher*, starring Gerard Butler as Sam Childers, the real-life rescuer of war-children in Sudan. The link between his name and his life mission struck me immediately.)

The Buffalo University professors refer to these preferences as *implicit egotism*. They argue that our social and life choices are grounded in our very identity, i.e. our name.

So the more we can identify personally with what is being said *and* who is saying it — as in a testimonial — the likelier we are to believe it.

And this takes us back to *personalising* our writing to our reader (Technique #1): the more our content and style chime with

---

6   'Narcissism beyond Gestalt and awareness: the name letter effect', *European Journal of Social Psychology*, 1985

their needs and preoccupations rather than our own, the more they recognise *themselves* in our words, the likelier they are to do what we want them to do.

As Jozef Nuttin's 1985 article suggested, our name is probably the sweetest-sounding word in our lexicon. If ever you doubt the power of personalising your writing to your reader, consider this: if you were scanning a document and you happened to spot your own name in the text, would that make you more or less likely to read it? The answer is obvious.

INDUSTRY RECOGNITION

Every industry around the world has its prestigious awards, usually culminating in a lavish, black tie event held in a plush venue *compèred* by a celebrity.

In the UK creative industries (advertising, media), it's the D&AD Awards and their famous wood, graphite, yellow, white and black pencils for different award categories. In architecture, winning the RIBA (Royal Institute of British Architects) Stirling Prize puts your practice on the map, while the *PRWeek* Awards are acknowledged as the most prestigious in the public relations and communications sector.

BAFTA (British Academy of Film and Television Arts) hosts annual awards for film, television, children's film and television, and interactive media. On the other side of the Pond, of course the Oscars recognise the highest achievements in the film industry, while the Antoinette Perry Award for Excellence in Theatre, better known as the Tony Award, recognises achievement in live Broadway theatre.

In the world of law, firms seek industry recognition through the legal directories, like Chambers & Partners and The Legal 500. These publications rank lawyers up and down the country and categorise them by location and specialism. They're considered so important that firms employ whole teams to draft directory submissions. Whatever your field, being recognised by your peers (and competitors) as an expert is the ultimate accolade and another form of evidence that reassures potential buyers and investors of the calibre of your product or service.

MEDIA COVERAGE

Media coverage matters, because it builds trust and awareness. Whether it's a book review in an industry journal, a radio interview or a TV programme broadcasting your views on a topic, it gives you or your brand status. That an editor considers you newsworthy reassures other people that you are worth paying attention to.

STATS AND OTHER EVIDENCE

Using numbers to back up your argument can weigh heavily in your favour, especially with people whose enquiry is more factual than emotive.

Customer satisfaction levels, products sold, conversion ratios, win-rates, average number of complaints, staff turnover, revenue growth, defect rates, productivity, delegate numbers, attendance, bookings, carbon emissions, fuel efficiency, exam grades — the list is endless.

My daughter's secondary school emailed me recently, inviting me to set up a small monthly standing order for the school's lottery, the proceeds of which they use to buy equipment and fund special projects. The first prize is £100 (about US$150), with 60 members (staff, parents and others associated with the school) signed up.

The email told me that the money raised enables them to continue to fund things like cultural trips (and indirectly benefit my own daughter); it gave me examples of equipment (table tennis tables, basketball hoops etc) that they've been able to afford; it gave me the names of the previous months' winners. But it ended with a number that I found quite compelling: it reminded me that my chances of winning the school lottery are a mere 1 in 60, while the UK's National Lottery are an infinitesimal 1 in 14,000,000!

As I said in Technique #6, Grab Your Reader's Attention, quantifying a fact implies authority, precision and completeness; it reassures your reader that you know what you're talking about.

There are other types of evidence we can use, too.

In Technique #4, Establish Your Objective, I cited the case of Debbie N, a family friend and single mum with a young son who has lived in the same area of London as us for 25 years. Debbie had learnt that the municipal authority was planning to re-house her in a distant part of the borough. This would have taken her away from her local support network, making it hard for her to keep her job and look after her three-year-old son.

So she contacted her local Member of Parliament (MP).

Besides arguing in her email to the MP that the move would jeopardise her job and compromise their lifestyle, she added a simple piece of evidence: she listed the local streets where her support network lived, all a stone's throw from her home.

Though not convincing on its own, this was another small brick in the argument that she built to be housed in the area that she knew and loved. The email worked: the MP lent his support to her claim and the Housing Department let her stay where she was.

CONSUMER REVIEWS AND RATINGS

When we're in the market for buying a book on a particular topic, we tend to scan the options on Amazon and narrow them down to a couple of titles. We'll click on 'Look inside' to get a feel for the scope of the topic, as well as the level and style of the writing. If that all checks out OK on both books, we'll read the reviews to see what others have said about the book. If book A has 23, five-star reviews, but book B only has seven, we'll tend to go for book A (unless book B covers a particular aspect of the subject that book A doesn't). So the reader reviews act literally as the 'title decider', the clincher, the tie-break. It's the differentiator that helps us decide, and feel good about the decision.

Recent studies have shown that 95% of shoppers consult customer reviews, while more than 86% of consumers say that reviews are an essential resource when making purchase decisions.

The reason for this is that we tend to trust other consumers more than we trust brands. Of course the manufacturer or brand ambassador is going to say nice things about their product or service, because they want us to buy it. But people who have already read the book or bought the toaster have no vested interest in giving a biased view: they can record their own experience with impunity.

This, then, is the value to us of product reviews: consumers can tell us what they think freely, without fear or favour.

SOCIAL MEDIA LIKES, SHARES AND RE-TWEETS

Whenever someone clicks on the thumbs-up icon, shares your content with their network or forwards your tweet to their followers, they're endorsing you and your content. They're saying 'Check this out: it's worth your time and attention'. The more this happens, the higher your profile, the more others will see you as a 'player' in your field and start looking out for your stuff. In this attention war we're all fighting in, you become a destination for others; they seek out your content. You'll become what Daniel Priestley refers to as a 'KPI': not a Key Performance Indicator, but a Key Person of Influence.

FOOD FOR THOUGHT

Re-check a live or recent piece of communication. Are you using the power of third-party evidence (e.g. testimonials, references, stats, social media endorsement) to persuade your reader to do whatever you are asking them to do?

The bottom line: we feel safer and are therefore likelier to do something if we see other people who we think are like us doing it too. Give your reader the evidence — in the form of social or numerical proof — that convinces them they're making the right choice.

rhetorica® Technique #9:

Tell Your Reader A Story

To paraphrase Robert McKee's encyclopedic book on screen-writing, *Story*[7], in one global day, how many stories do we tell and consume?

Imagine the pages turned, films and TV shows screened, plays performed, bed-time stories read, garden-fence gossip peddled, print and digital news broadcast, blogs posted, books published, speeches made, anecdotes told. Our appetite for stories is insatiable.

Why?

Because stories connect. They connect us with the storyteller or the hero by making us think and feel, by taking us to a different place in our imaginations, by immersing us in a new world. If Mind Maps® engage our brain, then stories fire our soul.

For millennia, communities have passed down knowledge and experience through stories. Before we could write, stories told orally transferred learning and wisdom from one group or

---

7   Methuen, 1999

generation to another. We're hard-wired to respond to a good story.

I'm speculating here — and a linguistics expert would probably have my guts for garters — but I wonder if there is a connection between the phrase 'relate a story' and the concept of 'relationship'.

'Relate' is from Middle French *relater*, to 'refer or report' and directly from the Latin *relatus*, the past participle of *referre*, to 'bring back' or 'carry back', hence 'reference'. Perhaps this hints at an early human understanding of stories' ability to give us reference points to live by, to connect and deepen generational knowledge and values, to remind us what it means to be human. As the American literary theorist Kenneth Burke said, 'Stories are equipment for living'.

We can use stories to tell people who we are, to show them what we believe in, to inspire them to action, to model new behaviours. We can use stories to touch, heal, inspire or change others. We can use stories to persuade.

WHAT'S THE SCIENCE BEHIND STORY?

Stories are persuasive because — if they're well told — we get swept up in them, we lose ourselves in them. The key word is *transportation*.

Psychological research on persuasion (Green & Brock: *Journal of Personality and Social Psychology*, Vol 79(5), Nov 2000) suggests that stories which *transport* us to an imagined world or a new way of thinking or feeling are likelier to be persuasive. Inside the story we're less likely to notice things that don't match up with our everyday experience. When we're wrapped up in a story, we're less aware of being persuaded: the message slips under the radar. Stories disarm us.

It's as if there's an inverse correlation between our emotions and our intellect: the more we're swept up in the story's emotional journey, the less intellectually critical we become. We lose the ability to argue against the story's premise or the information presented in it. Our critical faculties are disabled. We suspend disbelief, perhaps because we know that our enjoyment comes not from the intellectual stimulus, but from the emotional transportation.

Research has also shown that stories can influence people's attitudes (Green & Brock, 2000; Marsh, Meade, & Roediger 2003; Mazzocco et al., 2010; Prentice, Gerrig, & Bailis, 1997). For example, Green and Brock (2000) found that readers who got involved in a story reported attitudes more congruent with the story's theme.

In one study, Green and Brock (2000; Study 4) asked participants to read a short story about an Eskimo boy and his dog who become stranded on an ice floe. The boy and his dog have no food or supplies. During the night, both consider killing the other for food, but do not, out of loyalty to and love for each other. In the morning, the boy and dog are rescued. Green and Brock found that readers, questioned after reading and buying into the story, subsequently attributed greater importance to the values of friendship and loyalty.

USING MINI-STORIES TO PERSUADE

If you're writing a film script, a novel or a play, then you need to understand the classic three-act structure of any story, as defined by our rhetoric friend, Aristotle (I can highly recommend *Story* by Robert McKee and Joseph Campbell's classic, *The Hero with a Thousand Faces*, about story archetypes and the Hero's Journey). But I suspect you're more interested in telling a quick anecdote to make a point, give an example, send a message. You want to use mini-stories to persuade.

Marketers have known for years that stories are a powerful tool for persuading people. Stories are easier to understand than statistics, and more engaging than dry facts. They breathe life into information, give meaning to data, make the abstract concrete.

When someone in a business setting asks me how I transform people's writing, after giving them a few facts about my business I sometimes tell this (true) story:

STORY — HOW DO I DO WHAT I DO?

A couple of years ago I ran a writing workshop in Houston for a team of oil & gas engineers. They'd learnt my writing techniques in the morning and, in the main exercise of the day, they had to apply them to their own writing. One particular guy — a big, burly, bearded Texan in the front row — was visibly struggling. He kept shifting on his seat, chewing his pencil, writing something then crossing it out, sighing, puffing his cheeks out. His whole body was a picture of frustration.

I sat down with him and asked him what the problem was. He told me he couldn't put into words what was in his head. I asked him to explain it to me as if he was explaining it to his mum, his wife or his daughter. Although his explanation wasn't crystal-clear, it was much better than what he'd written down. 'Write that,' I said, 'and treat that as your first draft. Then you're off and running.'

He went very quiet for a moment and looked down. I was shocked: his eyes were welling up. Something about his writing must have shifted for him there and then, like someone had flicked a switch in his brain. He turned to me with a big, teary smile on his face and gave me a bear-hug that almost killed me.

That's why I say that my writing training makes grown men cry.

HOW DO WE WRITE POWERFUL STORIES?

Most stories begin with a temporal phrase, i.e. a phrase that locates the action in a time and a place, the most famous one, of course, being *Once upon a time...* We only need to hear or read those four words and we know we're about to be told a story.

A long time ago, in a galaxy far, far away...
(Star Wars)

It was early morning on 8 July 2010 in Helmand Province, Afghanistan...

It was April in Paris...

In this partial extract from their appeal letter, here's how a charity, Blind Veterans UK, used a story to raise donations:

STORY — A SOLDIER FIGHTS FOR THE REST OF HIS LIFE

It was early morning on 8 July 2010 in Helmand Province, Afghanistan, when Lance Bombardier Rob Long[8] took a step that would change his life forever.

Rob's Special Observer party walked right into an IED. The improvised explosive device killed his friend Bombardier Sam Robinson instantly and horribly wounded Rob himself.

The blast was so powerful it ripped Rob's helmet in half.

---

8   Rob gave me his personal permission to use his story. He is about to open a new chapter in his life, entering full-time education. He is a remarkable, courageous human being. Thank you, Rob.

Several weeks later, Rob woke up in a hospital bed in Selly Oak, Birmingham, to be told he had lost one eye and was blinded in the other. At just 22, his life as a Forward Observer in the British Army's (Sphinx) Special Observation Battery was over.

It fell to me to help Rob pick up the pieces of his shattered life and learn to live again. As a Rehabilitation & Training Manager for Blind Veterans UK, part of my job involves visiting newly blinded service men and women during their first few days in hospital after being brought back from the frontline.

I vividly remember the first day I met Rob. Although he was clearly scared, he was determined he wasn't going to be beaten. With enormous courage, he got out of bed, put his arm on mine and began to learn the skill that would change his life forever. I helped him learn how to use a white cane — and those faltering steps that day were the start of Rob's long road back to independence.

Today, Blind Veterans UK needs your help to support thousands of others like Rob. Please give what you can.

Yours sincerely

Julie Shales
Rehabilitation & Training Manager
Blind Veterans UK, Sheffield

Quoting Rob himself — 'They took my eyes, but they'll never take my independence' — the appeal is so much more powerful for focusing on a real person. The story of Rob's wounds, his initial despair and his courageous determination to make the best of his life with the help of Blind Veterans UK[9] affected me in a way that a factual statement of their work could never have done.

THE FOUR ELEMENTS OF STORY

The Blind Veterans UK appeal illustrates the four vital ingredients of any story:

1. **Protagonist, or Hero.**
   This is the main character, who needs to be likeable but wilful, and must have a conscious desire or goal. Rob is the hero of the story (but is aided by the charity); his goal is to regain his independence.

2. **Predicament.**
   The challenge or barrier blocking the hero from their goal, e.g. a physical, mental, economic, social or environmental hurdle. Rob's predicament is his sudden loss of sight and his resulting dependence on others.

3. **Narrative.**
   Also known as the plot, this recounts what happens and where; it gives the story its context and setting. This is the story of what happened to Rob and his sudden life change.

4. **Resolution.**
   How the Hero overcomes their predicament and moves to a new, better reality. Although Rob's predicament may never be fully resolved, we learn of his determination not to be defeated and to regain his independence.

From Shakespeare's *Hamlet* to Arnold Schwarzenegger in *The Terminator* series, all good stories embrace these four elements.

---

9   www.blindveterans.org.uk

STORIES OF LEGENDARY CUSTOMER SERVICE

In the canon of customer service, stories convince more than any corporate mission, vision or values statement. Here are a couple from Nordstrom, the US fashion retailer, whose tales have become the stuff of urban legend:

STORY — DIAMONDS ARE FOREVER

In 2011, a woman trying on clothes at a Nordstrom store in North Carolina lost the diamond from her wedding ring. She was distraught. A store security worker saw her crawling on the floor under the racks of clothes. He asked what was going on, then joined the search. After they came up empty, the employee asked two building-services workers to join the search. They opened up the bags of every vacuum cleaner in the store... and found the diamond.

STORY — 'NO TYRES? NO PROBLEM!'

A customer in Fairbanks, Alaska, wanted to return two car tyres bought a while ago from another store on the same site, but which had since closed down. The Nordstrom sales clerk looked up their price and gave the man his money back!

As a Customer Service champion once said, 'Customer service isn't about telling people how awesome you are. It's about creating stories that do the talking for you.'

WE NEED TO TELL MORE STORIES IN BUSINESS

The Nordstrom customer service legends are only a short hop away from being business case studies — literally stories that make the case for hiring that company or buying their goods. When a commercial organisation talks about facing a serious challenge and turning it around, they automatically use the four story elements, or should do. Consider how a bids & tenders consultancy describes its service in two very different ways:

Without a story	With a story
We are a leading, international bids & tenders consultancy that helps clients around the world to win lucrative contracts.	Last year the senior partner of a regional law firm called us up in a panic. His firm's Business Development (BD) Director had been taken ill, two weeks before the deadline to submit a bid to retain a contract as incumbent legal advisers to a key account. To add to the pressure, the client's General Counsel had told the firm he would switch advisers if the bid response was not up to scratch — then brought the deadline forward by three days.
We have ten offices around the world: five in the UK, three in the US and two in Asia.	We mobilised quickly and sent one of our senior bid writers to the law firm, but it soon became clear they needed more help. The bid was in a mess, with the inexperienced bid team chasing its tail. The messaging was unclear; the draft response lacked structure and was poorly written.

We employ 27 highly experienced bid writers full-time, who have won more than £1bn worth of bids in the voluntary, public and private sectors and will bring penetrating, unparalleled insights into your bid responses.	We took two of our bid writers off other, smaller jobs and sent them, plus a graphic designer, to the bidding firm. Working alongside the managing partner, his bid manager and the small BD team, our staff worked around the clock, even sleeping in their offices for three nights to make best use of the limited time available. (They also contributed to the local economy with midnight orders to Domino's Pizza.)
We offer clients bespoke, world-class training in the latest bid writing techniques that will raise your tender win-rate.	We helped the law firm pull together a decent response, which hit the client's buttons and addressed their main concerns. It was a close-run thing, but the client re-appointed the firm for another three years.

The left-hand column — full of boasting, promises and grandiose claims — is all about the supplier (note over-use of the word *we*). The right-hand column brings those claims to life by offering us a real example. It's much more convincing, because the plight of the failing bid will resonate with a reader in a similar situation. They will put themselves in the story as they read it.

This is what stories do: they allow us to *show* rather than *tell*. In turn, this helps us avoid the Hysterical School of Writing exemplified in the left-hand column above.

Sadly, this hyperbolic style seems to be infectious, because it isn't confined to the corporate world. When applying to university, for example, in their Personal Statements British students tend to *tell* more than they *show*:

Ever since I was a young boy I have wanted to study mechanical engineering at Bristol University, as I am passionate about this enthralling subject...

I was at nursery school when I discovered that I wanted to be an international litigator specialising in competition law...

I will bring unrivalled passion to your world-class degree course and offer you deep, penetrating insights into the subject with my limitless energy and enthusiasm...

This is telling, not showing; this is emoting, not evoking. This is poor writing.

Tell a story instead that *demonstrates* your passion for the subject:

STORY — 'WHY MECHANICAL ENGINEERING IS A NATURAL FOR ME'

As a young boy I used to take things apart. I started with my PlayStation and Wii games consoles, but — to my parents' horror — soon progressed to household appliances like kettles, irons and fridges. Eager for me not to destroy our home completely, my father encouraged me to work with him on his motorbikes, which at the time he raced. I quickly became so proficient that he used me rather than the local garage to strip down and tune up his bike before an important race.

When Design Technology (DT) was added to the National Curriculum, it was a natural choice for me. Working with a range of materials, from metals to plastics, and developing my workshop skills, I revelled in solving practical problems. I love finding out how things work.

So, when I found out about the Bristol University mechanical engineering degree at the open day and met the lecturers and tutors, it was as natural a choice for me as my decision to do DT.

STORIES MAKE IT PERSONAL

When applying for a job or employment of any sort, spouting an impressive track record or top credentials usually isn't enough. In my experience, hirers also want a sense of the applicant as a person; they want some human colour.

Compare these two versions of a covering letter for a CV, written by a student applying for an ODI Fellowship (the Overseas Development Institute is a UK think-tank on international development and humanitarian issues):

VERSION A

Dear Sir,

By the end of this letter, I would like to convince you that my experience, knowledge and current skill-set make me an ideal candidate for the ODI Fellowship. Your 'desirable' requirements include a demonstrable interest in development. I do not have an interest in development — I have a calling for it.

I decided to study Economics at Warwick University, to learn how to approach development issues through an evaluative, scientific framework. The course had mathematical rigour in both micro- and macro-economic theory. Having written my undergraduate dissertation on the impact of microfinance loans on poor households in Bangladesh, in which I used econometric techniques and micro-economic theory, I also have a strong grasp of applying theory in a development context. I graduated from Warwick with upper second class honours, and moved to an MSc in Population & Development from the London School of Economics.

Yours faithfully
Katia J

VERSION B

Dear Sir,

By the end of this letter, I would like to convince you that my experience, knowledge and current skill-set make me an ideal candidate for the ODI Fellowship. Your 'desirable' requirements include a demonstrable interest in development. I do not have an interest in development — I have a calling for it.

In 1997, walking through a market in Pakistan, gripping my mother's hand, I was approached by a young girl, similar to me in many ways: we both had roots in the same country; we were both about the same age; and we were both walking on the same street. Yet she was alone, barefoot, hungry and asking me for 'just one rupee'. For years after this, I simply couldn't understand how we could have so much in common, but lead lives that were worlds apart. Since then, I have tried to understand how this disparity came about and how we can work effectively towards a world without such stark inequalities.

So I decided to study Economics at Warwick University, to learn how to approach development issues through an evaluative, scientific framework. The course had mathematical rigour in both micro- and macro-economic theory. Having written my undergraduate dissertation on the impact of microfinance loans on poor households in Bangladesh, in which I used econometric techniques and micro-economic theory, I also have a strong grasp of applying theory in a development context. I graduated from Warwick with upper second class honours, and moved to an MSc in Population & Development from the London School of Economics.

Yours faithfully
Katia J

By telling the story (the italicised text in Version B) of what ignited her passion for international development, Katia (not her real name) adds a human element to what would otherwise be a run-of-the-mill covering letter. It reinforces her claim that she has a calling for the field, not just an interest in it. To the ODI evaluator, it *shows* her passion for the subject, so she doesn't have to use that hackneyed word in her letter. And it gives a sense of her as a real person, rather than merely a candidate. It makes the letter distinctive because it gives it *personality*.

FOOD FOR THOUGHT

If your communication lacks impact — maybe it's too dry, too factual, too academic, too theoretical, too cerebral — humanise it. Tell a story.

The bottom line: ever since humans learnt to use words, they have told stories. Good stories well told bring ideas to life, give concepts form, evoke emotions, ignite imaginations. Sometimes it's not about persuasion. Sometimes we just want to tell a story around the dinner table or the camp fire that restores our faith in people. Here's one, reproduced with the kind permission of *The Big Issue*, a wonderful, weekly publication sold by homeless people to the general public on the streets of Britain:

COMMENT OF THE WEEK

Thanks to a vendor's help, small change was no big issue

Had a heart-warming experience last week. As I headed into Sainsbury's with a Spanish friend I had given a lift to, I stopped to buy a Big Issue from the vendor near the entrance. I was aghast when I put my hand in my bag and found my wallet wasn't there. The vendor and my friend watched, concerned, as I mentally retraced my steps before realising it was safe in another bag. I apologised to the vendor for being unable to buy a magazine while my friend got a trolley designed for wheelchair/Zimmer frame users. I asked him why he was choosing that one. He said he didn't have a £1 coin for the other sort. At that point the vendor held out a £1 coin and said we could return it to him when we finished our shopping which, of course, we did. By this time we had change and were also able to buy a copy of *The Big Issue*. Simple story but the engagement was heart-warming and we all benefitted.

Sally Guyer, Cambridge

rhetorica® Technique #10:

Pre-empt Likely Objections

Imagine you're attending a job interview.

You're wearing your favourite dress or suit, you've had a good night's sleep; you feel great. You're meeting the Head of Recruitment. You shake their hand, make strong eye contact, flash them your winning smile. 'Good morning. Nice to meet you. Thank you for seeing me.' You're going to have to build rapport quickly.

With your CV in front of them, they tell you about the job and what would be expected of you. You note their body language, their vocal intonation, the words they emphasise, when they look at you and when they look away. Although you speak well about your academic, sporting and work-based achievements, you sense their concern about your lack of experience. You ask the question and, sure enough, they *are* concerned about your inexperience in similar roles. You've uncovered a major objection.

Instead of being defensive about it, however, you meet it head-on. You thank them for being honest with you. Then you give brief examples of how your motivation to excel, your ability to learn fast and your experience of a key aspect of the role in a different job would compensate for your inexperience.

Now try doing all that in a letter or email.

In a written communication you have none of the non-verbal cues available to you in a face-to-face meeting. You can't gauge the other side's response — their body language or their tone of voice. But you *can* do your research, put yourself in their shoes and brainstorm their likeliest objections to giving you the job.

Then you can raise those objections rhetorically in your copy… and answer them. This is salesmanship in print.

The theory is that, if you've answered all their objections by the end of your communication, they'll be convinced.

I say 'theory', because they may be *intellectually* convinced, but conviction is about more than intellect. In an interview scenario, for instance, the recruiter will still want to meet you in person, especially if they're recruiting for an important role. They'll want to be sure that you're the 'right fit' with them and their organisation; that you're on their wavelength and share similar values. With a big commitment like giving someone a job, both sides need to be as certain as they can be that they're making the right choice.

Generally, the bigger the commitment you're asking for from your reader — whether money, time, information or good will — the richer the contact they will want with you. The ultimate 'rich' contact is meeting you face-to-face: that gives them the panoply of verbal and non-verbal signals that support or undermine your message. But that's not always possible: if your readers are spread around the world, you may only have recourse to the written word to convince them.

THE TWO INGREDIENTS OF CONVICTION:
LOGIC AND EMOTION

I closed Technique #4, Establish Your Objective, by asserting that logic makes people think, but feeling (as in the second F of F.F.A.) makes them *act*. When we want to convince someone to do something by addressing their likely objections, we're using the same premise. We're satisfying their pre-frontal-cortex, rational need to see that there's no logical foundation to their concerns. But we're also satisfying their reptilian brain that subliminally is asking 'Will I be OK with you?', 'Will you give me what I want?', 'Will I be safe?'

These are basic, survival-oriented questions that — assuming the answers satisfy us — give us the emotional reassurance we need in order to do what the writer is asking us to do.

That's why I believe that almost all objections are rooted in one emotion: fear.

We're scared of making the wrong decision, of not getting the result we want, of being inconvenienced or compromised, of losing value. And for 'value' read money, time, information, advantage, reputation, status, influence or control.

Here are the most common objections, their underlying concerns and some suggestions for dealing with them:

Objection & how it's expressed	The underlying concern	Objection-handling tactics
Price: 'You're more expensive than your competitors.' 'We can't afford you.'	Fear of not getting the value for money they seek or are promised.	Re-state their objectives and the personal/professional value to them of meeting those objectives. Then describe in exhaustive detail how your product, service, approach or team will deliver against each objective. Relate the benefits of hiring you to the value they seek, using concrete, relevant examples.
Time: 'We don't have the time for this.' 'This is not the right time.' 'The timing's not right.'	Fear of losing this finite resource and not getting enough value from their time investment. Fear of not getting the result(s) they seek.	Show them that the longer they wait, the more value they're losing. Show them where and how the market is moving: they need to keep up. Give them a clear timeline so they can plan how to allocate their resources. Break the work down into manageable, realistic phases that make sense to them and their situation. Explain how easy it is to get started and the 'quick wins' possible early on.

Status quo, complacency: 'We're happy with our current provider, thanks.' 'We're not looking to change right now.'	Fear of changing to a new provider who is an 'unknown quantity' and may not give them the value they seek.	Give examples of major changes in their industry in the last five years and their positive impact. Tell them about improvements that their competitors have made/are making. Raise the prospect of being left behind. Arouse their competitive instinct. Offer compelling credentials that make them feel that, if they do switch to you, you'll be 'a safe pair of hands'.
Inexperience: 'We haven't worked with you before.'	Fear of not getting the result(s) they seek. Fear that you won't understand the particular issues of their industry or field, that you'll be out of your depth.	Give them compelling evidence (references, case studies, testimonials, quotes, industry awards, books etc) that you are as good as you claim to be. Let them speak to referees, previous/existing clients. But always be honest about what you can and cannot do.

Do-ability:	Fear of not	Give them evidence of
'Will you be able to deliver?'	getting the result(s) they seek.	similar projects or contracts you have delivered — and the results your clients obtained. Show them you have both the capacity and capability to help them.
		Strong evidence will temper their uncertainty.

You can see how many times the word *fear* occurs in the middle column.

The best (and maybe the only) way of overcoming fear is to build trust. What follows are three scenarios where I deal with three unspoken but likely objections, in a bid to build the reader's trust:

Scenario 1: A website selling mentoring services to people interested in property investment.

Likely objection from potential client: 'How do I know that your property mentoring service is good value for money?'

First, please read some of the testimonials from delighted customers; these are real, recent and relevant. Second, you can speak to any of our referees and previous clients about their experience with us and the results we've helped them achieve. You'll find their contact details underneath their picture, so you can call them directly.

Then try our property advisory service for 30 days free of charge, with a dedicated advisor to guide you. If at the end of 30 days you don't feel you've had the value you were hoping for, then you've lost nothing and gained some free advice. But if you do feel you've had value, you can subscribe to the service with total confidence.

Scenario 2: Letter from a home-owner, Paula, to her next-door neighbour, Anne, about impending works to build a conservatory extension on the back of their house.

Likely objection from affected neighbour Anne: 'I'm worried that the noise and inconvenience of the works next door will disturb me and my family.'

Dear Anne, it was good to chat to you the other day about our building works, which are due to begin 1 September. From your questions, I gather that you are worried about the impact of the works on you and your family. I quite understand; I would be the same if the roles were reversed.

Inevitably, there will be some noise and disturbance; I'm afraid we can't avoid that. But I just want you to know that we will be doing at least five things to keep this to a minimum:

1. *The builders will start early (0630) and leave the site at 1700 every day;*

2. *They will leave the pavement in front of both our houses clean and tidy, especially the kerb in front of your driveway;*

3. *They will give you at least a day's notice of large deliveries of building materials that could obstruct your driveway and/or create a mess;*

4. *There will be no weekend working;*

5. *The builders will do as much drilling/sawing inside the house as they can, to keep the noise and vibrations down.*

Please let me know if there is anything else you would like us to do, to minimise the impact on you and your family.

Kind regards
Paula

Scenario 3: Application to a London Local Authority for funding to run a personal development programme for troubled teenagers, focusing on self-esteem, trust and forgiveness.

Likely objection from Local Authority evaluator: 'How will you engage distractible teenagers on the subject of forgiveness?'

You might be wondering how we're going to engage disengaged teenagers on the subject of forgiveness.

The module starts with a brief, facilitated discussion of 'What is forgiveness?'

Then the mother of a 15-year-old girl killed by a hit-and-run driver will talk to us about coming to terms with her daughter's death and forgiving the driver who hit her. The driver who killed her daughter — shackled and in prison uniform, as he's still serving his sentence for reckless driving — will be standing beside her and will share with the group how it feels to be forgiven.

We will end the session with feedback from the group on how what they've heard has changed their understanding of forgiveness.

PRODUCT OBJECTIONS VS SERVICE OBJECTIONS

If you're selling an object, like a car, a cooker or a candle, it's the same product for everyone. It may not be the same experience for everyone, but your reader can test-drive the car, touch the cooker or smell the candle; the product is concrete, not abstract. Any objections they have will be based on a real rather than an imagined experience.

If, however, you're selling life coaching, management consulting or marriage guidance, there's no physical product. It's an expert service that represents a more subjective choice based largely on the personal chemistry between you and them. The stronger the rapport between the two of you, the better their experience is likely to be; the value is in the quality of the relationship. So, if possible, the best option is to allow them to meet you and experience that chemistry (or lack of it) themselves.

That's why I offer potential clients a free 'taster' of a few of my writing techniques: they get value from the session, but more importantly they get to know me and get the emotional reassurance — in most cases — that I'm OK and that their people and their investment in me will be safe. And if they do still have objections, they can air them there and then.

Now, meeting your reader or prospect face-to-face may not always be possible.

I live in London, so it's neither practical nor cost-effective to offer tasters to companies outside the UK. But Skype or video conferencing is an acceptable substitute: seeing you address their concerns on screen goes a long way to reassuring them that you're trustworthy. Combine that with evidence in the form of case studies, testimonials, references, books, industry awards or press coverage (Technique # 8, Convince Your Reader With Evidence) and you'll be well on your way to convincing them.

FOOD FOR THOUGHT

Review a recent piece of persuasive writing where you argue for a course of action or a decision from your reader. They're likely to have objections to your argument. Do you know what they are? And if so, are you addressing them in detail?

If you're struggling to come up with meaningful objections, that suggests you don't know your reader well enough. Find out more about them. If possible, speak to them; get to know them. Ask them directly what their concerns are. If they hesitate, prompt them by saying 'One of the common questions that people have about my service is... [price, timing, process etc]. Does that concern you, too?' You can only deal with their particular objections when you know what they are. Then deal with them either directly in your copy or in the form of FAQs.

The bottom line: when persuading someone to change their mind and their behaviour, put yourself in their shoes. Pre-empt their likely objections and answer them in detail. This will satisfy their need both to rationalise their decision and to feel understood. Remember that the primary emotion driving most objections is fear. The more they know, like and trust you, the safer they will feel and the likelier they will be to do what you want.

rhetorica® Technique #11:

Write Plain English

An important concept in English is *register*, a scale of the formality of writing.

As you can see below, the scale has 'FORMAL' at the top and 'SLANG' at the bottom. Let's use *money*, a classic, mid-register word, as an example and populate the register with synonyms for it:

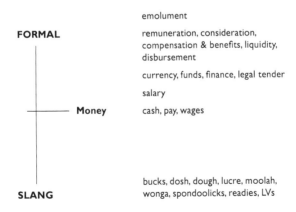

emolument

FORMAL

remuneration, consideration, compensation & benefits, liquidity, disbursement

currency, funds, finance, legal tender

salary

Money — cash, pay, wages

bucks, dosh, dough, lucre, moolah, wonga, spondoolicks, readies, LVs

SLANG

In the upper reaches of the register we have words like *remuneration, consideration, liqudity, finance, 'comp & bens'*, with *emolument* off the scale. In the middle of the register, words like *cash, pay* and *salary* accompany *money*, while in the depths of the slang world we have words like *wonga, dosh, dough, lucre, moolah, spondoolicks, LVs* (Lager Vouchers), depending on which side of the Pond you sit.

What do you notice about the formal, upper register words?

They're longer and harder to spell. They're less well understood. They're more elevated, exclusive, solemn and aloof; they risk alienating your reader. Acting more as a barrier than a bridge, upper register words put distance between you and your reader. And that's bad news if you're trying to persuade them to do something they wouldn't otherwise do.

There's another problem with formal language.

When I run this register exercise in my writing workshops, there's always a titter or a chuckle when someone suggests *wonga* or *dosh*. Whether or not it's due to people feeling naughty using slang in a 'professional' context, there's an emotional response in the form of laughter. But when someone says *remuneration* or *emolument*, there's silence. Why?

Because upper register language is emotionless. It's technical language that's been dehumanised: it's lost its human voice.

For instance, which of these two sentences sounds more human?

> *We will undertake collaborative in-depth ideas review and enhancement*

> or

> *We'll look at the ideas with you and improve on them together*

I know which style I'd rather read.

Conversational, mid-register language brings our reader close and helps establish an intimacy with them. It helps them warm to us on a human level.

But wait: there's something else (you'll need money for this)!

Besides losing emotion and pushing the reader away, something else happens to language as we move up the register.

I'll give you a clue: take some money out of your pocket, wallet or purse and play around with it. Touch it, smell it, look at it. If it's a coin, tap it on the table; if it's a note, wave it in the air. Could you do that with any of the upper register words? No. As we move up the register, language not only becomes longer, harder to spell and more sophisticated; it also becomes more *abstract*.

So what?

Abstract language is harder for the human brain to process. Adopting a formal, high-register style makes your reader work hard to get your meaning. The harder they work, the likelier they are to stop reading.

Mid-register = plain English

Generally, the best place to be is in the middle of the register. Where upper register lingo is derived from Latin and Greek, mid-register is the home of good old Anglo-Saxon, aka plain English, or PE. Here the words are shorter, pithier and universally understood. Everyone knows what *cash* is and what it does; not everyone knows what an *emolument* is — and why should they?

Here are some PE alternatives to the most common examples of posh-speak:

Posh-speak	Plain-speak
assist	help, aid
attain	reach, meet, hit (e.g. a goal)
beverage	drink
commence	start, begin, kick off
construct	build
depart	leave
disseminate	spread, share, give out
prior to	before
optimal	best, ideal
purchase	buy
request	ask
requirement	need
significant	big, important, meaningful
terminate	end, fire, kill
transmit	send
utilise	use, apply

Easy, isn't it? (To get your plain English black belt, remember to take the quiz at the end of the chapter.)

THIS IS NOT ABOUT DUMBING-DOWN

Sometimes when people look at the list above, they bemoan the loss of linguistic sophistication and accuse me of wanting to dumb-down their writing.

Nothing could be further from the truth.

The content of your writing must still be top-notch, i.e. engaging and relevant, considered and intellectually rigorous. But that doesn't mean you have to convey it in formal, upper register language. The real challenge in writing is to articulate complex ideas so simply — but not simplistically — that your reader 'gets' them in one go. For me, that's the Holy Grail of writing.

PLAIN ENGLISH ISN'T JUST SIMPLER: IT'S GOT MORE KICK

Besides the obvious benefit of clarity and readability, there's another reason to use plain English over formal language: it has more impact. Because it's concrete and more visual, it has greater emotional effect. It packs more of a punch.

So you could say,

> *The Engineering division has reduced its budget for next year*

but if you wanted more impact you'd say,

> *The Engineering division has slashed its budget for next year*

You can't picture a 'reduction' because it's an abstract concept, but you can picture a sword slashing something or someone in half.

Take the sentence,

> *This law will negatively impact on our profits.*

Does that have emotional kick? Not really.

The phrase *negatively impact* is ambiguous: it could be a huge impact or a tiny one. And it's weasel-worded, hedging-your-bets, sit-on-the-fence, non-committal language. If you wanted much more impact, you could say:

> *This law will cripple / crucify / wreck / ruin / maim*
> */ destroy our profits.*

But if you think that's a bit over the top and you want to be more measured, you could say:

> *This law will hurt / damage / harm our profits.*

Can you hear and feel the difference between all those alternatives and *negatively impact*?

These are 'power words'. Of course, your choice of which word to use comes down to your judgment as the writer, what you judge as accurate and appropriate for your reader and achieves the intended effect. We don't have to get hysterical about it.

To borrow the advertising slogan of a well-known UK brand of DIY products, plain English is Ronseal language: 'It does what it says on the tin'. It's immediate and your reader gets your message in one go. They'll love you for it.

Plain English gives your writing personality

Nothing kills personality quicker than formal language.

Sophisticated, high-register, polysyllabic words stifle our voice in a vice of formality. The further away we move from the human voice, the less we connect with our reader. And the weaker the connection, the less persuasive our writing. Plain English, on the other hand, frees our writing and allows our human voice to come through, because that's how we speak when we're conversing with other humans. Conversational writing makes it easier for the reader to hear us speaking through our words. This is the auditory aspect of writing that many people neglect — and why ROL (Read Your Writing Out Loud, Technique #18) is such a great way of checking your writing and assessing your tone of voice.

There are three elements to good writing: great content, clarity, and the missing ingredient, personality. In the next Technique, Vary Your Register And Tone Of Voice, we look at how to write with personality.

Plain English is not *always* the right choice

You will have gathered by now that I recommend plain English as your default style. There are occasions, however, when it serves us to use more formal, technical language.

For instance, if *remuneration* is precisely the right *technical* term for your context (e.g. if you're addressing a company's Remuneration Committee), or if that's the term that will resonate with your reader, then that's the word you must use. But if all you mean is, 'You'll get more cash in your pocket at the end of the month', then use the everyday English equivalent.

Similarly, if you were writing to or for the UK's MOD (Ministry of Defence) or the US Department of Defense, you might use technical, military language that resonated with them, e.g. 'deploy troops in a theatre of operations'. This is formal, emotionless, upper register language appropriate for that particular context.

If, however, your readership included non-military readers, such as members of the public, you might talk instead about 'putting boots on the ground'. This is mid-register, concrete, visual language: we can visualise a soldier in full kit fighting in a desert *wadi* or trudging through a fetid jungle. It creates a mental image.

STILL UNSURE ABOUT PLAIN ENGLISH?

If you're still not convinced about the merits of plain English, consider this: it's much quicker and easier to draft in plain English than in higher register language, because that's how we speak. It's ironic that some writers reach for Roget's Thesaurus every five minutes to move their writing *up* the register, while their reader will reach for the Oxford English Dictionary to bring it back *down* so they can understand it! Talk about not connecting with your reader.

A poll taken at Stanford University[10] found that 86.4% of the students surveyed admitted they had used complicated language in their academic essays to make themselves sound cleverer.

Nearly two-thirds answered 'Yes' to the question, 'When you write an essay, do you turn to the thesaurus to choose words that are more complex to give the impression that the content is more valid or intelligent?'

The Stanford University study found that needlessly complex text makes the author seem *less* intelligent to the reader, while expressing complex ideas simply makes them seem *more* intelligent.

But research has shown that people equate a large vocabulary with intelligence. So why don't long, complicated, high-register words impress and persuade the reader?

---

10 'Consequences of Erudite Vernacular Utilized Irrespective of Necessity: Problems with Using Long Words Needlessly' *Applied Cognitive Psychology* 20: 139–156 (2006); Daniel M Oppenheimer, Princeton University'

I think there are four reasons:

1. Everyone knows that complicating the simple is easier than simplifying the complex. Readers resent writers who leave it to them to do the hard work, i.e. discern the structure, translate the language and decode the message.

2. Readers don't feel connected to writers who are more interested in impressing them and showing off than in genuinely communicating with them. These writers are serving their own needs rather than the reader's.

3. Simple language is easier to process than complicated language: high-register words impede understanding. The risk is that the reader misses the point and isn't inspired to action.

4. Writers sometimes use language to conceal rather than communicate, making readers understandably suspicious of fancy, high falutin' words. 'What's this writer trying to hide, and why?' Business-speak is particularly guilty of this.

On that note, here's a humorous look at translating coded phrases from corporate annual reports into plain English, borrowed from an April 2007 article in *The Sunday Telegraph*[11]:

---

11 'How to deconstruct the annual report', Sylvia Pfeifer, Business section, *The Sunday Telegraph*, 8 April 2007

Annual report version	What it really means
XYZ plc's performance this year can best be described as 'mixed'.	We had an *annus horribilis*.
In the summer of 2015, John and I agreed that he would step down as chief executive.	We had a major row and I won.
There is increasing global competition for access to opportunities.	We are fighting off the Chinese and Indians.
We have operations in emerging markets where political, economic and social transition is taking place.	We work in dictatorships with riots in the streets.
If we do not apply our resources to overcome the perceived trade-off between global access to energy and the protection or improvement of the natural environment, we could fail to live up to our aspirations of no or minimal damage to the environment.	We may have a few oil spills here and there.
Actual results may differ materially from those expressed in forward-looking statements.	Don't blame us if the future isn't as rosy as we predicted.

FOOD FOR THOUGHT

Test your plain English mastery with this quiz. Write a plain English word or words next to each of the following (answers overleaf; don't cheat now!):

1 henceforth ....

2 hitherto ....

3 facilitate ....

4 contiguous to ....

5 in addition ....

6 notwithstanding ....

7 *prima facie* (Latin) ....

8 in respect of ....

9 aggregate ....

10 ascertain ....

11 eradicate ....

12 modify ....

13 endeavour (verb) ....

14 *per annum* ....

15 requisite ....

16 peruse ....

17 occasion (verb)   ....

18 retain   ....

19 pursuant to   ....

20 think outside the box   ....

The bottom line: a C.R.I.S.P. (sorry, another dreaded acronym) summary of the benefits of mid-register plain English:

<u>C</u>larity: 100% clear to 99% of your readers; they'll get it in one go.

<u>R</u>eadability: simple words in short sentences are less taxing on the reader's brain and therefore easier to read.

<u>I</u>mpact: evocative, emotive, vivid, visual 'power' words live here.

<u>S</u>peed: it's faster to draft in plain English, because that's how we speak.

<u>P</u>ersonality: simple language allows the author's voice to come through.

PLAIN ENGLISH QUIZ: ANSWERS

1	henceforth	from now on
2	hitherto	up to now, up till now
3	facilitate	support, help, ease, make easy
4	contiguous to	next to
5	in addition	and, also, what's more
6	notwithstanding	despite, although, even though
7	*prima facie* (Latin)	at first sight / glance ('*prima facie* evidence')
8	in respect of	about, on, of, for ('a study in respect of obesity')
9	aggregate	total
10	ascertain	find out
11	eradicate	rid, get rid of, remove
12	modify	change
13	endeavour (verb)	try
14	*per annum*	a year
15	requisite	needed, required
16	peruse	read, browse
17	occasion (verb)	cause

18	retain	keep
19	pursuant to	under ('pursuant to the contract')
20	think outside the box	brainstorm, think creatively / laterally

rhetorica® Technique #12:

Vary Your Register And Tone Of Voice

In the previous chapter, we established the concept of register as the scale of formality of your writing. Plain English sits slap-bang in the middle of the register and I waxed lyrical about its advantages.

The best writers, however, aren't slaves to the mantra of plain English.

They vary their register. Great writers, like the journalists who write for *The Economist,* bounce up and down the register all the time:

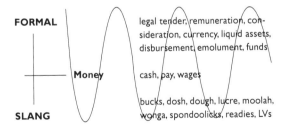

FORMAL

Money — legal tender, remuneration, consideration, currency, liquid assets, disbursement, emolument, funds

Money — cash, pay, wages

SLANG — bucks, dosh, dough, lucre, moolah, wonga, spondoolicks, readies, LVs

They have the intellectual confidence to refer to the UK's immigration policy as *barmy*, Thabo Mbeki as *prickly* or the future as *dicey*. They're not afraid to use *dosh* and *remuneration* in the same paragraph. Sometimes they vary the register within a phrase, let alone a sentence or a paragraph.

When John McCain ran against Barack Obama in the 2008 US presidential election, *The Economist* published an in-depth profile of McCain where they described him as having 'a blokeish persona'. *Blokeish* is an Anglicism from the slang word *bloke*, meaning laddish or 'one of the boys', while *persona* is an upper register Latin word meaning 'public face' or 'mask'.

The point about mixing up the register is that it makes your writing more interesting; you can achieve different effects than if you stay rooted in one level of formality. Another way of putting it is that it allows you to write with *personality*.

In practice, what does writing with personality mean?

I think it takes two forms:

1. expressing a strong point of view in a human voice;

2. using levity, humour or irreverence.

PERSONALITY: EXPRESSING A POINT OF VIEW IN A HUMAN VOICE

Whatever your topic, you have to have an informed point of view on it. Like Martin Luther nailing his list of grievances to the door of a Catholic church in 1517, you have to take a position and be prepared to defend it. That's how you influence people's perception of you.

In this article from the *Evening Standard* in August 2013, the authors (four prominent UK Liberal Democrat politicians) open — and end — with a clear opinion on Syria's use of chemical weapons:

> *Large-scale use of chemical weapons is a war crime and a crime against humanity...*

> *... But we are certain. The law is the law. No two nations have the right to prevent it from being enforced. For the humanitarian sake of the Syrian people — and in defence of peace and stability around the world — these laws must be upheld.*

No bet-hedging or fence-sitting there.

In business too, where everyone is clamouring to be heard in a crowded marketplace, companies that express a strong point of view in an authentic, human voice are more likely to be listened to. Organisations that can't break out of corporate-speak and won't adopt the conversational voice of the marketplace will be ignored.

The point about writing with personality is that you have to take risks and that's hard for risk-averse organisations. If you're more concerned with your Compliance or Legal department than with your reader and you're not prepared to go out on a limb in both style and content, your communications will be bland.

And I'm not talking here about 'oh-my-God-I-can't-believe-they-said-that-I'm-going-to-write-to-the-Ombudsman' risks, either.

Many of my clients hail from professional services (e.g. lawyers, architects, engineers, accountants, auditors), and they increasingly seek my help with writing blogs on industry developments or new legislation. They want their writing to stand out, to be distinctive, to be 'edgier'. In other words, they want to take risks. In a recent workshop with a law firm client on writing blog posts, I innocently suggested that using contractions (e.g. *can't, won't, I'd, she'll*) would help them sound more approachable and less corporate.

Almost in unison they threw their arms up in horror and said in all seriousness that that would be going too far. 'Too risqué!' one of them cried. If that's how inelastic their risk taking is, then they will struggle to write stuff that people want to read. The only exception to that rule is if they publish content that's so good or so fast (e.g. being the first law firm to respond to new legislation) that readers will tolerate their über-formal style.

PERSONALITY: USING LEVITY, HUMOUR OR IRREVERENCE

Where taking a position on a topic is about content, this type of personality writing is more about style.

Compare, for instance, two alternative openings to a law firm blog post:

> *17 October the FCA published, unannounced, a new Press Office Handbook on its website.*

> *The other day the FCA published (very quietly) a new Press Office Handbook on its website.*

The first version is neutral, matter of fact, strait-laced, one-dimensional. The second version is more casual (*the other day*) and has more interesting sub-text: the bracketed stage whisper *very quietly* hints that the FCA wanted the publication of the Handbook to go unnoticed, to slip underneath the radar. Those two words in brackets intrigue us and spike our curiosity in a way that the first version doesn't.

The Economist is masterful at writing with personality. Take a look at this apology from a few years back:

Unintentional class war: in some copies of this week's edition we somehow managed to misspell 'bourgeoisie' on the cover of our special report celebrating the rise of the middle class in the emerging world. Apologies to all concerned, although if you go to Highgate cemetery, you may well hear the sound of an elderly German chuckling.

[Karl Marx is buried in Highgate cemetery, London]

In the world of consumer branding — arguably all about personality — corporations like Kellogg's and Coca-Cola have always spent big on advertising and promotions to embed brand personality in consumers' minds. But smaller, more entrepreneurial brands can't afford to do that, so they use their packaging instead. Look at Innocent, the UK 'smoothie' brand that has taken packaging copy to new heights with personality and humour:

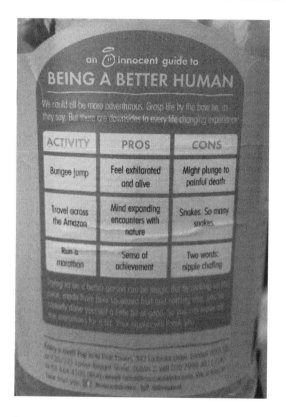

Quirky, funny, maverick, mischievous, off-the-wall — you may not like it, but it's hard to ignore. That's personality.

Besides register, we need to vary our tone of voice, too

If register is the scale of formality of our writing, what is tone of voice?

In my writing workshops someone usually pipes up with 'arrogant' or 'pompous' or 'friendly' or 'warm'. These are adjectives describing a tone of voice; they don't define what tone of voice is.

Here are various definitions I've heard over the years:

'It's not what you say; it's how you say it'

'... the mood your writing creates'

'... the décor of your writing'

'... how you come across'

Given that readers hear our words in their heads when they read our stuff, my favourite is:

'How our writing sounds to the reader
and makes them feel'

Firstly, as I've said before, there's an *auditory* element to writing: we hear the writer's words in our head, as if they were speaking to us. We don't *read* tone of voice; we *hear* it. That's why ROL is such a powerful way of checking how your writing will sound to your reader (see Technique #18).

Secondly, we're back to the 'F' word: Feeling.

Do we want our reader to feel bored, irritated, alienated? Or engaged, excited and connected to us? If you recall from Technique #4, Establish Your Objective, logic makes people think, but emotion makes them act. When we strike a tone of voice that makes our reader feel good about us and the content, they're more receptive to our message.

Sometimes changing one or two words makes all the difference to tone of voice.

Spot the difference between these two versions of the same email from a senior Learning & Development manager to her team. This...

> *A workshop will be held next Monday for staff, to help
> participants improve their writing skills.*

... or this?

> *We are running a workshop next Monday, to help us
> improve our writing skills.*

Besides turning the passive voice of the first version into the active, the personal *we* and *us* in the second version are more inclusive, consensual and collegiate than the impersonal *staff* and *participants*. By placing herself on the same level as her team, the manager shows humility. The second version is also engaging because its tone of voice is more conversational.

When you read something addressed to you and other readers, do you feel like a 'participant' or 'staff member', part of a 'customer base' or a 'demographic'? No, you feel like you, a unique, special individual, and you want to be spoken to in that way.

And if we really wanted to blow the minds of our risk-averse brethren in the example above, we could use a contraction and say *'We're running a workshop next Monday... '* But for some that would be beyond the pale.

FOOD FOR THOUGHT

To achieve interesting effects in their writing and keep their reader engaged, good writers vary their register. Unconfident writers tend to stick in the same place on the register — usually formal. Could your writing benefit from being bolder in your choice of register?

Complete the 'Informal' and 'Formal' columns for each word in the table below and see how your word-choice multiplies when you do so. You'll find suggested answers overleaf.

Informal	Normal	Formal
	car	
	drunk	
	tired	
	poor	
	steal	
	difficult	
	happy	
	sad	
	wife	
	write	
	money	
	sleep	
	destroy	

The bottom line: online or offline, writers who compete for eyeballs and attention are mistaken if they think that great content clearly written will cut it. The missing ingredient is personality. Writing with personality is about expressing an informed point of view or adopting an irreverent tone of voice that surprises the reader and gets them coming back for more. Even when writing about serious things, like presidential campaigns or industry regulators, serious doesn't have to mean dull.

(Suggested) answers

Informal	Normal	Formal
banger, ride, jalopy, motor, wheels	car	automobile, vehicle
pissed, rat-arsed, hammered, wasted, four sheets to the wind	drunk	inebriated, intoxicated
knackered, wasted, toast, pooped, shagged	tired	fatigued, exhausted
broke, brassic, hard-up	poor	impecunious, impoverished
pinch, nick, half-inch, lift	steal	thieve, misappropriate, embezzle
hard, tough, big ask	difficult	complex, complicated, problematic, challenging
over the moon, chuffed	happy	delighted, jubilant, ecstatic, joyful
down (in the dumps), bummed out, blue, pissed off	sad	depressed, in low spirits, sorrowful, melancholy

missus, other half, trouble & strife, her indoors	wife	spouse, partner
jot, pen, scribble	write	correspond, draft
dosh, dough, bucks, dollar, wonga	money	revenue, remuneration, income, funds, finance, liquidity
nap, kip, shut-eye, 40 winks, doze	sleep	slumber, repose
ruin, wreck, trash, break, smash, mash up	destroy	annihilate, obliterate, decimate, devastate

rhetorica® Technique #13:

Omit Needless Words

When I ask people on my writing workshops what they most want to improve about their writing, nine times out of ten they say 'conciseness'.

The solution is simple: the single best way to write concisely is to omit redundant or needless words.

Words that add no value, content, meaning or information elongate your sentences and puff up your text. Remove them. When we write concisely, we create prose that is taut, lean and delivers what I call 'cut-through'. Its ASL (Average Sentence Length, in words; see Technique #20) will also be lower.

That's it. I could end this chapter here (I'm serious), but my publisher would get annoyed.

In a moment I'm going to break needless words down into five discrete categories, but before I do, here's a taster:

Wordy	Concise
The team is made up of five people	The team comprises five people (37% shorter) N.B. comprises, NOT comprises of; you could also say consists of, but that's longer.
A significant reduction in incidents	Far fewer incidents (40% shorter)
The majority of students	Most students (50% shorter)
Have a detrimental effect on	Hurt, harm, damage (80% shorter)
Staff training is reviewed on a weekly basis every Tuesday	We review staff training every Tuesday (40% shorter)

NEEDLESS WORDS, CATEGORY 1: WAFFLE, WORDINESS AND WIND

This irksome condition afflicts writers with little or nothing to say, so they pad out and puff up their writing with words that add neither impact nor meaning. Otherwise known as PAs, or Pompous Asses, they use 15 words where five would do. Here's what I mean:

At this present moment in time we are currently offering free coffee	We are offering free coffee (We are offering is in the present tense, so you've already told the reader that the action is happening now, making at this present moment in time and currently redundant)
Send it to our office, which is located in the city of Boston	Send it to our Boston office (Most people know Boston is both a city and a location)
In the interim period between the years of 1999 to 2004	Between 1999 and 2004 1999–2004 (interim means 'between' and your readers will recognise those numbers as years; you can also use an en-dash — not a hyphen! — between the years)

NEEDLESS WORDS, CATEGORY 2: TAUTOLOGIES

A tautology is the use of two different words or phrases to convey the same idea. For example:

A pair of twins: this is either redundant or ambiguous. Is it two or four people?

Blue in colour: as opposed to blue in weight? But as a client once said, it could be 'blue in content'.

Seventeen years of age: thank you, but we know that *years* are a unit of age.

Totally unique: something is either unique or it's not; it's binary, like pregnancy or a switch. A woman can't be 'slightly pregnant', nor can a light switch be 'slightly on'.

Surrounded on all sides: *surrounded* means 'on all sides'.

Close scrutiny: by definition *scrutiny* means close examination, so *close* is redundant.

Close proximity: as above.

Past experience: by definition, *experience* is always in the past.

Future plans: by definition, all *plans* are future-based.

Safe haven: if somewhere is unsafe, it's not a haven!

A sudden bang: a loud bang doesn't go off gradually; 'Bang!' is by definition a sudden, loud noise.

NEEDLESS WORDS, CATEGORY 3:
LAZY SUPERLATIVES

Novice writers often think that they improve their writing by qualifying nouns with hyperbolic adjectives. Here are a few:

A grave crisis
(this is arguably a tautology too: you can't exactly
have a trivial or light-hearted crisis)

A bad accident

A severe problem

A terrible emergency

A superb decision

I call these 'lazy superlatives' because the writer is trying to add impact, but at the expense of more useful information. Good writers seek to *inform*, rather than emphasise:

An <u>*economic*</u> *crisis*

A <u>*road-traffic*</u> *accident*

A <u>*debt*</u> *problem*

A <u>*humanitarian*</u> *emergency*

A <u>*unanimous*</u> *decision*

NEEDLESS WORDS, CATEGORY 4: ABSTRACT NOUNS

What's the trouble with abstract nouns? They don't convey concrete things, but intangible, intellectual concepts, which are harder for the reader's brain to process. As we saw with register in the previous chapter, the more abstract your writing, the harder your reader has to work.

Common abstract nouns include *extent, degree, nature, fashion, way, manner, basis*. We can often remove them:

Now you see them...	Now you don't...
This happens to a significant <u>extent/degree</u>	This happens a lot/often
This report is of a confidential <u>nature</u>	This report is confidential
Staff of XYZ organisation always operate in a professional <u>fashion/way/manner</u>	Staff of XYZ organisation always operate professionally/are professionals
We publish this bulletin on a quarterly <u>basis</u>	We publish this bulletin quarterly

NEEDLESS WORDS, CATEGORY 5: NEEDY VERBS

These are emotionally dependent verbs that crave company in the form of an adverb (a word that qualifies a noun, like *noisily* in the first example):

The cup falls noisily to the floor

The share price will drop sharply

She got less and less angry

Profits are climbing steadily

He's changed the team completely

She examined the document closely

But English is full of resilient verbs that can do the job on their own, without annoying adverbs hanging on their every word:

The cup crashes/clatters to the floor

The share price will plummet

Her anger abated/subsided

Profits are soaring

He's transformed/revolutionised the team

She scrutinised the document

(Please turn over for **Food for thought**...)

FOOD FOR THOUGHT

Here's a list of 15 wordy phrases. Substitute them with one or, at the most, two words. You'll find the answers overleaf.

1   for the purpose of   ....

2   for the reason that   ....

3   in order to   ....

4   in the event that   ....

5   on the grounds that   ....

6   in respect of   ....

7   face up to   ....

8   except in a very few instances   ....

9   in short supply   ....

10 during the time that   ....

11 due to the fact that   ....

12 notwithstanding the fact that   ....

13 involve the necessity of   ....

14 make the acquaintance of   ....

15 prior to   ....

The bottom line: we need to remember the advice offered by William Strunk and EB White in *The Elements of Style*[12]. Writing shouldn't contain unnecessary words or a paragraph unnecessary sentences 'for the same reason that a drawing should have no unnecessary lines and a machine no unnecessary parts'. Omitting needless words is about economy of language. If a word ain't doing a job, remove it.

FOOD FOR THOUGHT: SUGGESTED ALTERNATIVES

1	for the purpose of	to, for e.g. *for the purposes of training and quality*
2	for the reason that	because, as, since, due to, owing to, thanks to, for
3	in order to	to
4	in the event that	if, when, in case, should e.g. *Should he arrive on time...*
5	on the grounds that	because, as, since, due to, owing to, thanks to, for, based on
6	in respect of	about, re, regarding (but over-use the latter and you risk sounding pompous)
7	face up to	face, confront, accept, address, own, tackle, admit, recognise, deal with, acknowledge
8	except in a very few instances	mostly, usually, typically, commonly, normally

---

12 Longman, 2000

9	in short supply	lacking, limited, rare, scarce, sparse
10	during the time that	while, when
11	due to the fact that	because, as, since, due to, owing to, thanks to, for
12	notwithstanding the fact that	despite, although, even though
13	involve the necessity of	require, need, involve, demand, call for, entail, warrant, mandate, merit, justify (these last ones are more formal, so beware)
14	make the acquaintance of	meet
15	prior to	before

At this point someone often pipes up, 'Yes, but if you want to impress the reader, surely it helps to use big words?'

'What's the risk in using big words?' I reply. 'The risk is that you obscure your meaning and lose your reader. And will they be impressed then?' (The room usually falls silent here.)

What *will* most impress your reader?

Cracking content conveyed so clearly and simply that they get it *in one go*. That will blow them away, partly because it's rarer than hens' teeth. The belief that using long, fancy words will impress your reader and get them to do what you want is *a big myth*. Good ideas and great content stand up on their own: they don't need puffing, tarting or dressing up.

rhetorica® Technique #14:

Use More Verbs Than Nouns

A serious disease afflicting writing these days — especially corporate/institutional writing — is nounitis, the excessive use of nouns.

First diagnosed by Rupert Morris in *The Right Way to Write*[13], it's infectious and widespread. But it's also curable. The cure? Use more verbs. Here's an example:

> *The key to our rapid expansion is the provision of health and fitness advice to our members.*

Sounds clunky, doesn't it? Identify all the nouns (underlined below) and you'll quickly see it's suffering from acute nounitis:

> *The <u>key</u> to our rapid <u>expansion</u> is the <u>provision</u> of <u>health</u> and <u>fitness</u> <u>advice</u> to our <u>members</u>.*

It's bogged down by seven abstract nouns, two of which end in –sion, so it sounds repetitive and samey (plus the only verb is *is*).

---

13   Piatkus, 1998

Remind me, what's a noun?

It's a naming word, or a person, place, object (e.g. a chair) or idea (e.g. freedom). The problem with nouns is they just sit there naming stuff, but don't *do* anything or go anywhere. If the universal cure for nounitis is to use more verbs, what's a verb? It's an action or doing word. So apply the cure to Version 1 and you get:

> *We have expanded rapidly because we provide health and fitness advice to our members.*

That's better: we've got two verbs in *expanded* and *provide*, and we've replaced the SOW (Severely Over-used Word) *key* with *because*.

But there's a problem with this version: another big fat SOW is running around. *Provide*. I'd put good money on the fact that *provide* — and all its horrible relations — is the single most over-used word in writing, bar none. Not only that, but it carries the nounitis virus. Whenever you use the word, you have to follow it with a noun, e.g. *we provide advice, we provide support, we provide briefings, we provide guidance*. Just use the verb: *we advise, we support, we brief, we guide*. It works in most contexts. So you're banned from using *provide* in the next and final version.

> *We have <u>expanded</u> rapidly because we <u>advise</u> our members on health and fitness.*

That's now better with two strong verbs (underlined), but it's still a bit vague, isn't it? 'Health and fitness' is a huge topic. So let's give the reader a bit more information:

> *We have <u>expanded</u> rapidly because we <u>advise</u> our members on how to <u>stay</u> fit and healthy.*

Adding a third verb in *stay* gives the sentence more fluency and the reader more information about the sort of advice the members will get.

We've cured the original sentence of its rampant nounitis. But — time permitting — we should always seek further improvements. Here are a couple of optional extras: contract *We have* to *We've*, to make it more conversational, and replace the three-syllable *expanded* with a one-syllable verb like *grown*. You end up with:

> *We've grown rapidly because we <u>advise</u> our members*
> *on how to <u>stay</u> fit and healthy.*

Voilà!

So how do you self-diagnose? How do you know if you've got nounitis?

Go through your text and note all the words ending in:

- tion (e.g. facilitation, implementation, collaboration, delegation)

- sion (e.g. conversion, provision, decision)

- ism (e.g. specialism, magnetism, terrorism)

- ity (e.g. capability, adversity, speciality)

- ment (e.g. management, judgment, assessment)

- ance (e.g. performance, maintenance, attendance)

- sis (e.g. analysis, diagnosis, paralysis)

- al (e.g. refusal, referral, proposal)

- age (e.g. wastage, appendage, verbiage)

- acy (e.g. advocacy, conspiracy, piracy)

- ure (e.g. departure, failure, enclosure)

- ing (e.g. landing, writing, feeding)

Take your writer's scalpel and lop off those endings (technically known as 'suffixes') to revert to the root verb. You win in two ways: you invigorate your writing by using more words of action/doing, and you make it briefer, as the verb is always shorter than its noun equivalent.

Here's another easy example for you:

An ad recently posted in a local rag reads:

> *The use of massage has been used for many years for the treatment of musculoskeletal problems…*
> (16 words)

Firstly, the author has needlessly repeated the idea of *use*. So let's omit the needless words, as per Technique #13.

Secondly, let's replace the noun phrase *the treatment of* with its verb equivalent, so the edited version would read:

> *For many years, massage has been used to treat musculoskeletal problems…*
> (11 words)

Not only have we cut the word count by 31% (11/16 x 100), but by using a verb (*treat*) we've made the sentence more vigorous.

Here's a lovely example from a law firm blog:

> *This may assist our arguments in favour of the*
> *deletion or amendment of the clauses.*

The three abstract nouns *arguments, deletion* and *amendment* bog
the sentence down. Use more verbs and say:

> *This may help us argue in favour of deleting or*
> *amending the clauses.*

Three strong verbs and you're cooking with gas.

STILL NOT CONVINCED ABOUT NOUNITIS? TRY THIS

An academic called Judith ignominiously won the 1997 Bad
Writing Contest. Here's one of her sentences, running to 94
words and stuffed with 30 abstract nouns (in bold):

> *The **move** from a structuralist **account** in which **capital** is*
> *understood to structure social **relations** in relatively homolo-*
> *gous ways to a **view** of **hegemony** in which **power relations***
> *are subject to **repetition, convergence,** and **re-articulation***
> *brought the **question** of **temporality** into the **thinking** of*
> ***structure,** and marked a **shift** from a **form** of Althusserian*
> ***theory** that takes structural **totalities** as theoretical **objects***
> *to one in which the **insights** into the contingent **possibility***
> *of **structure** inaugurate a renewed **conception** of **hegemony***
> *as bound up with the contingent **sites** and **strategies** of the*
> ***re-articulation** of **power.***

Qué? Abstract nouns are more taxing on the reader's brain than
concrete nouns, and concrete nouns are more taxing than verbs.
Not surprisingly, this passage gets a readability score of 0% (see
Technique #19, Score Your Readability).

Sorry, Judith, but it had to be done.

WHEN TO LIVE WITH NOUNITIS

Some industry terms don't benefit from being cured, however. In financial services, for example, 'risk management', 'asset & liability management' and 'asset allocation' are recognisable, shorthand phrases that everyone in that industry uses and broadly understands (also known as a 'term of art'). To dismantle them into verbs might cause confusion and stop reading flow.

FOOD FOR THOUGHT

Take a section or paragraph of one of your recent documents and identify all the nouns, i.e. person, place, object (e.g. sofa) or idea (e.g. democracy). Then replace as many as you can with verbs, as long as they don't change the meaning. Now read it out loud. Does it sound better or worse?

The bottom line: as long as you know the difference between a noun (a naming word) and a verb (an action word), you can cure your own nounitis quickly and easily. Nouns — especially abstract ones — make your writing longer and more turgid; verbs free it up, make it flow and give it vigour. What's not to like?

Write In The Active Voice

As insidious as nounitis, is the passive voice. It's crept into our words like a thief in the night. I call it the carbon monoxide of writing, the silent killer. Many people write in the passive voice and don't even know it.

HOW DO YOU FORM THE PASSIVE VOICE?

To cure your *passivitis*, you first need to understand its inner workings. Here's a simple example:

> *The dog bit her.*

The *dog* is the subject, *bit* is the past tense of the verb *to bite*, and *her* is the object, because she's the one who's been bitten. This gives us a declarative sentence: Subject – Verb – Object, meaning that that sentence is in *the active voice* (AV).

The passive version of the same sentence is:

> *She was bitten by the dog.*

Although grammarians give them different labels, as we move

from the active to the passive voice, the subject and the object effectively switch places. When we put the sentence above into the passive, the object *her* becomes the subject *she* (even though she's still the *logical* object, because she's the one who's been bitten). The original subject *The dog* becomes what's known as the 'agent' (the person or thing responsible for the action) and has the preposition *by* placed in front of it.

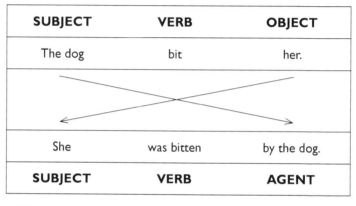

SUBJECT	VERB	OBJECT
The dog	bit	her.
She	was bitten	by the dog.
SUBJECT	VERB	AGENT

Table borrowed from *Oxford A–Z of Grammar & Punctuation*, John Seely, OUP 2013

What obvious difference between the two versions do you notice?

Yup, the passive version is longer, 50% longer in fact (six words vs four is an increase of half). And is there any difference in meaning? None. So if you're a fan of the passive voice, your writing will be 50% longer than it needs to be with no added value, content, meaning or information. And that's a big deal for any writing, especially if you're working within a strict word or character limit.

How else do the two versions differ? The passive one is less direct, more complicated and makes your reader's brain work harder to decode its meaning. In the context of one simple sentence like this one, you may think this is all a storm in a tea cup, but over a longer document it will make a big cumulative difference.

IT + PASSIVE: THE 'PASSIVE IMPERSONAL'

You can also form the passive with *it*:

It is believed that unicorns exist.

This suggests a widespread or established belief. But if you know who the unicorn-believers are, then use the active voice:

Our next-door neighbours believe that unicorns exist.

A delegate on one of my writing workshops made me laugh when we were discussing the passive voice. He said, 'It's a bit like this' and he proceeded to loop his right arm over the top of his head and scratch his left ear. It was a demonstrative, if slightly quirky, way of showing us how contorted and unnatural the passive voice is.

I'm advocating that you use the active voice much more than the passive. The active voice is briefer and forces you to state who is doing what to whom. Simple, clear, direct.

However, there are four occasions when it's OK to use the passive:

1. *To cover your backside or be less direct.* The passive voice lets you drop the subject, e.g. *She was bitten* is grammatically correct, but we no longer know who did the biting. So use the passive if you want to hide responsibility for something, or be less confrontational. For instance, you often hear government representatives after a disaster or scandal using language like '*Mistakes were made, targets were missed but lessons will be learnt*'. We don't know who made the mistakes and

missed the targets and who will learn the lessons. Classic, butt-covering language courtesy of the passive voice.

Another scenario is where you don't want to ruffle feathers. A client was slow paying one of my invoices recently. I knew it wasn't a problem with my service; it was more to do with their disorganisation. I could have used the active voice, as in 'Tom, you haven't paid my invoice yet', which could have sounded confrontational. Instead, I said, 'Tom, my invoice hasn't been paid yet'. (They paid a few days later and my relationship with Tom was unscathed.)

2. **To emphasise the object.** As the passive forces you to put the object at the front of the sentence, this automatically emphasises it. Based on the theory of primacy, the first word or idea in a sentence gets the reader's attention. So we might say *The red-head in the spandex suit was bitten by the dog.*

3. **When the subject is unknown.** Use the passive voice if you don't know who or what the subject is, typically in the commission of a crime:

A murder was committed
(we don't know who dunnit)
A shot was fired
(we don't know who the shooter was)
Our friends were burgled
(they don't know who burgled them)

4. **When the subject is unimportant.** *The file was uploaded to the server* and *The meeting was convened for Tuesday* are classic examples of the subject not mattering. It's immaterial who or what uploaded the file; it was probably an automatic process anyway. And does it matter who convened the meeting? These are examples where the *action* is more important than the *actor*.

VOICE VS TENSE

People sometimes confuse *voice* with *tense*, but they're two different things. The voice of a sentence is binary: it's either active or passive. A tense, however, locates an action in time, e.g. *We are being offered a discount* is in both the present tense and the passive voice; *we were offered a discount* is in the past tense and the passive; *we will be offered a discount* is in the future tense and the passive.

Sorry if you already know this, but some people think you can't change tenses in the passive; you can. So, to revert to our original example, you can just as easily say

> *She is being bitten by the dog*
> (present passive)

as

> *She will be bitten by the dog*
> (future passive)

as

> *She would be bitten by the dog, if the dog*
> *was off its leash*
> (conditional passive)

FOOD FOR THOUGHT

If you haven't already done so, run a Spelling & Grammar check on your document. This will highlight all the passives and give you the option of turning them into actives.

If you'd like to know what proportion of your sentences are in the passive voice (a useful stat to have), then you're going to have to read Technique #19, Score Your Readability. The readability stats calculate this for you. Ideally your passive score should be 0% — unless you're writing a crime report.

The bottom line: if you want your writing to be briefer, more direct and more dynamic, make the active voice your voice of choice. (And stop scratching your left ear with your right hand.)

rhetorica® Technique #16:

Dramatise Your Writing

There are points in our writing when we need to add some drama and spike the reader's attention. Here are five devices you can use:

DRAMA DEVICE #1 — CUTTING A DASH

The em-dash is a simple punctuation mark that can add spice to your writing. Use it for your punchline or to add a twist of lime at the end of your sentence:

> *High-achievers don't watch TV*
> *— they're too busy achieving.*

> *The young boy recognised the old man*
> *— it was his father.*

> *Bi-sexuality is great — it doubles your chances*
> *of a date on Saturday night.*

My advice on how to use the em-dash? Sparingly. If you insert it into every other sentence, you'll irritate the hell out of your reader.

And don't confuse the em-dash (—) with the en-dash (–), which, as you can see, is shorter. We use the en-dash to convey a range of values, e.g.

0900–1700, 2m–7m, 13–17 November etc

Worst of all, don't use a hyphen (-) instead of a dash. We use dashes to connect or separate *phrases* and *sentences*, as above; we use hyphens to connect or separate *words*, e.g. semi-circular, half-hearted, anti-Apartheid. They do different jobs.

DRAMA DEVICE #2 — STARTING SENTENCES WITH *AND* AND *BUT*

You can.

Despite what your primary school teacher drummed into you, it's grammatically OK.

You were probably told: 'Never begin sentences with a conjunction (a joining word) like *And* or *But*.' But sometimes they're the perfect way to switch from one topic to another. And you can do that efficiently by using a single word.

Separating the two clauses that *And* or *But* would normally join together calls attention to the new sentence created and spikes the reader's interest.

Here's what Webster's *Dictionary of English Usage* has to say about *But*:

> *Part of the folklore of usage is the belief that there is something wrong in beginning a sentence with But: many of us were taught that no sentence should begin with 'But'. If that's what you learned, unlearn it — there is no stronger word at the start. It announces*

> *total contrast with what has gone before, and the*
> *reader is primed for the change.*

I like that idea: a simple word priming the reader's brain for a change in tone, content or concept. Here's another example:

> *The law has changed. The RSPCA [Royal Society for the*
> *Prevention of Cruelty to Animals] can now undertake the*
> *biggest animal rescue ever. But we need your help.*

It's a pattern-breaker, a change of direction, sudden and abrupt, that wakes the reader up. Pick up any issue of *The Economist* and I guarantee you will find more than one sentence beginning with *And* or *But* in the leader article alone. If it's good enough for them, it's good enough for me.

However — and it's a big *however* — if there's a good chance of your reader having a stroke when they see a sentence beginning with a conjunction, then don't do it. You always have a choice. Just know in your very being that it's grammatically acceptable to do so.

DRAMA DEVICE #3 — USING POWER WORDS

I touched on this in Technique #11, Write Plain English, but it's worth repeating.

'Power' words are everyday, conversational, mid-register words that have greater emotional impact than their more formal counterparts. This is because, like all plain English words, they're concrete and visual; we can see them in our mind's eye. For example, we could say:

> *Public sector budgets have been heavily **reduced** this year.*

But if we wanted more of a reaction, we could say:

> *Public sector budgets have been **slashed** this year.*

Slash is more visual, more violent, more shocking (and we lose the adverb *heavily*, too).

Another example:

> *Profits have **fallen significantly** this quarter.*

But this is more powerful:

> *Profits have **plummeted** this quarter.*

And we lose the word *significantly*, so we gain brevity.

Or we could say:

> *Profits have been **dented/knocked/bashed** this quarter.*

We can all picture something being dented, knocked or bashed; the sentence doesn't force us to process an intellectual abstraction.

Or:

> *Accessing the internet on my new phone **uses lots of** battery.*

But I prefer:

> *Accessing the internet on my new phone **hammers** the battery.*

Again, we all know what a hammer looks like, so we can picture a battery being smashed with one; our brain conjures up that image quickly and easily.

The closer to the middle of the register you go, the less formal your language and the closer you get to real-life language that readers can relate to. Not only is plain English simple and clear, it's also more visually evocative and therefore more powerful.

DRAMA DEVICE #4 — PLACING YOUR POWER WORDS

Once you've decided which power word to use, you need to know where to put it.

Where's the hotspot of any sentence? Where will your power word most affect the reader?

Imagine that the line below represents a sentence: it doesn't matter how long it is or what it's about. We know that most sentences begin with a capital letter and most end with a full-stop. With a big, fat, bold X, mark where on this line you would place your power word:

A ————————————————————————

Based on the theory of *recency* — that the last thing the reader sees will most affect them — the hotspot of any sentence is the very last word:

A ———————————————————————— **X**

If you wanted to stress the word *free*, for example, you might say:

> *For the next seven days we're offering this service* **free**.

If you wanted to stress the word *die* (a terminal word if ever there was one), you might say:

> *If you don't sell now, the business may* **die**.

If you wanted to stress the word *now*, you might say:

*The time to act is **now**.*

THIS WORKS FOR SENTENCES AND PARAGRAPHS, TOO

The idea of holding our chilli peppers back to the end applies equally to the sentences of a paragraph and to the paragraphs of a document section.

But if you can't or don't want to place your power word at the end, where's the next best place? The beginning! Based on the theory of *primacy*, the very first word or group of words that the reader reads will stand out:

A X————————————————————————

To reverse the above examples, we could say:

Now is the time to act.

Unfortunately, if you try it for the other two examples, you end up sounding like Yoda from *Star Wars:*

Free will be our service to you.

Die the business will if sell you don't now.

So it doesn't always work. But it's better than burying your key word in the middle of the sentence, where it will get lost. (See, I've just done it there: I ended with *lost* to emphasise it.)

As with the em-dash, please don't try and shoe-horn your power words into the end or the beginning of every sentence, otherwise your writing will sound contrived and unnatural. Choose where and when you most need to deliver that killer blow to the reader. Wield The Force responsibly.

DRAMA DEVICE #5 — THE POWER OF THREE

Lists of three have been used in the earliest human communications, as they relate to how we process information. We recognise and respond to patterns, and three is the smallest number of elements needed to create a pattern. Known as a *tricolon*, this rhetorical device combines pattern and brevity to create impact:

The Good, the Bad and the Ugly
(1966 spaghetti western with Clint Eastwood)

'Veni, vidi, vici' — *'I came, I saw, I conquered'*
(Julius Caesar after invading Britain in 1st century BC)

Blood, sweat and tears
(misquoted from Winston Churchill, who actually said
'I have nothing to offer but blood, toil, tears and sweat')

One of the greatest orators and champions of rhetoric is Barack Obama, who often uses tricola. This is from his election night speech in November 2008 in a drizzly Chicago:

*'Hello Chicago. If there is anyone out there who still doubts that **America is a place where all things are possible**, who still wonders if **the dreams of our founders are alive in our time**, who still questions **the power of our democracy**, tonight is your answer.'*

Note, too, Obama's use of *anaphora*: repetition of words or a phrase ('who still...') at the start of a clause or sentence.

Further back in time, Elizabeth I's speech to her troops at Tilbury in 1588, as they prepared to face the Spanish Armada, uses two tricola in one sentence:

> '*Not doubting by your obedience to my general, by your concord in the camp, and by your valour in the field, we shall shortly have a famous victory over the enemies of God, of my kingdom, and of my people.*'

FOOD FOR THOUGHT

Read a recent document out loud. Are you instinctively using any of these dramatic devices? If so, great. Now you're aware of them, you can consciously choose which is the best to use where. And if you need inspiration, just read *The Economist* to see how they use the em-dash, how many sentences they launch with *And* and *But*, the number of power words they use, where they place them and the number of tricola. Study the best writers and your own writing will improve.

The bottom line: these five drama devices may sound like parlour tricks, but they work. If you did a functional MRI scan of your reader's brain as they were reading your copy, you'd want to see it 'lighting up', wouldn't you? That would mean vital parts of the brain were being engaged, with synapses firing like New Year celebrations. Using these devices will ignite your reader's synapses and keep them reading.

rhetorica® Technique #17:

Get Your Reader To Take Action

There's a difference between informative, influential and persuasive writing.

A flyer from my local municipal council about a new housing service is an example of *informative* writing. An article in *National Geographic* about white rhino poaching in South Africa that moves me and raises my awareness of the issue is an example of *influential* writing. But reading the website of a local maths tutor and calling her to find out if she can tutor my son is *persuasive* writing, because it's made me take an externally observable action.

If you want to change your reader's behaviour and persuade them to do something as a result of your words, you have to ask them to do it; coyness doesn't work. Make what you want them to do easy and clear by giving them a call to action (CTA) using a verb:

Get *your free ebook here*

Please **sign** the attached papers and **return**
them to me by Monday
Claim your early-bird discount by 12 Feb

Find your nearest pet store

CTAs typically come at the end of your document or email, because they're the point of your communication; the CTA is what your line of argument has been leading to. It's the A in F.F.A. (Technique #4, Establish Your Objective): the observable action you want your reader to take as a result of reading your words. It's the culmination of your persuasive efforts. And based on the theory of recency — that the reader most readily remembers and responds to the last thing they read — it makes sense to issue the CTA at the end. (This differs from *online* CTAs, as you'll see later in this chapter.)

I want to kick off by dealing with the three *worst* calls to action I see in letters and emails. I call them The Three Stooges:

Stooge #1: *Please don't hesitate to contact me.*

Stooge #2: *I look forward to hearing from you.*

Stooge #3: *Please get back to me at your earliest convenience.*

Stooge #1 is a boilerplate phrase that people trot out without thinking. But it introduces a negative concept and is expressed as a double-negative. If your offer is interesting to the reader, why should they hesitate? And why put them to the mental effort of decoding a double-negative? Why would you do that if you wanted a swift and positive response?

Just say 'Please contact me on *[telephone number]* if you'd like to know more about our around-the-clock weight loss helpline'. In other words, remind them of the benefits of your offer or service.

Stooge #2 is a bland, uninspiring catch-all. 'You can look forward to hearing back from me as much as you like...' might be the reader's response. And people generally don't care how you feel, or whether you're looking forwards or backwards.

Stooge #3 is another boilerplate phrase that gives your reader an easy escape. Their 'earliest convenience' might be never. Avoid it.

My take on getting a response from someone is that a 'No' reply is better than no reply at all. Don't know about you, but I can't stand radio silence. I'd rather hear bad news than no news. So, with communications where I seek a response, I add a rider to the call to action that goes something like:

> *Please contact me on [mobile number] by the end of next week if you'd like to know more about my bid-writing workshop.*
>
> *If I haven't heard from you by then, may I contact you the following week?*
>
> *Kind regards*
> *Scott*

I do this for three reasons:

- It lets them know that I'm serious about following up on their enquiry

- It gives me permission to chase them, without making me look like a pest or a stalker

- I retain some control in the relationship, as I'm not totally dependent on them to get back to me

You will have noticed, I'm sure, that the three stooges above lack one key element: a deadline. Without a deadline, a CTA is open-ended and lacks urgency; it allows the reader to push you down their agenda. Adding a deadline — as I did in the rider above — focuses their mind on a finite resource (time) and applies an important principle of persuasion: scarcity.

AROUSE DESIRE THROUGH SCARCITY

We can use the scarcity principle to make people want whatever we've got or to create a sense of urgency in them to get it.

One of the six universal principles of social influence identified by Dr Robert Cialdini, scarcity says that the less available something is, the more people want it. Rare or unique things hold greater perceived value for us; we want them more when we learn that they're available in limited quantities or for a limited time.

A petrol shortage is a good example. When its supply is restricted, demand typically soars, often with panic buying; the supply/demand equation loses its equilibrium. In that scenario a resource that many of us take for granted becomes more precious and we may be prepared to pay over the odds to get it. When normal supply resumes, petrol prices tend to return to their previous level.

Concorde is another example of scarcity, but here the 'resource' was finite.

When British Airways decided in February 2003 to ground the iconic plane after the terrible crash in 2000 over Paris, the sale of seats took off. And when its final flight was announced eight months later, thousands of people blocked a major motorway to say goodbye to the aircraft that they could have seen every single day for the previous thirty years.

USING SCARCITY IN YOUR CTA TO SELL A PRODUCT OR SERVICE

First, you need to convince the buyer of its benefits to them. Then tell them what is rare, unusual or unique about it.

In a proposal from an oilfield services company offering a new generation of drill technology to an oil & gas client, the author went to town on the benefits of increased rate of penetration, faster production and less 'red money' (written-off costs). But the clincher was in the last paragraph of the proposal:

> *We only have five of these drills available. Please get back to me by next week to sign the attached purchase order and ensure delivery in time for production on rig XYZ.*

You see, the benefits alone may not be enough to move the buyer to buy. They may still be unsure or scared of acting, so we can use scarcity to counter that inertia. Scarcity can push them to act by inducing in them a sense of urgency or a fear of missing out on something valuable.

CALLS TO INACTION

Sometimes the only response we want from the reader is to go away. We want to close the case, shut the enquiry, say 'No'. And Stooge #1 ('Please don't hesitate to contact me') can be quite good at doing that. Using such a clichéd close can give the reader the subliminal message that you're not really interested in hearing back from them. Try it and let me know how you get on. Alternatively, if your reader is a right pain in the backside, you can always refer them to a colleague you don't like, with the words 'Consider getting in touch with Mrs Palmer: she might be able to help you'.

Only joking.

GETTING PEOPLE TO TAKE ACTION ONLINE

When browsing online, we're fickle and unforgiving.

I'm not sure of the latest estimates of 'stickability' — how long (human) browsers spend on a site — but it's seconds, not minutes. If a site doesn't give us relevant information and a compelling call to action, we'll click away and go to the next link in the search results.

Busy readers seek reasons to stop reading our words, because they've got better things to do with their time. One such reason is being unclear about what to do next on a site. So every one of your web pages must have a CTA.

There are different schools of thought, however, about where to place it. Some say always put it 'above the fold' (what's visible in the browser window when the page first loads; also referred to as 'before the scroll', i.e. the portion of a webpage that's visible without scrolling). But it doesn't make sense to ask your reader to make a commitment until and unless you've shown them what they're going to get. That's fine if you're offering a simple product, like a memory card, a book or a key-ring. But if you're selling a high-value, complex service like a coaching programme or an external audit, a CTA above the fold could be premature and presumptuous.

Many websites offering complex services feature long copy running to several pages. Some readers may be convinced after 90 words, others after only 900. Sites like these issue CTAs at different points in the copy, so that a CTA is never more than a short scroll away. The key is to make it as easy as possible for the reader to act when they are moved to do so. Keep it simple:

Get a product demo

Subscribe to your client alerts

Download your free report

(Grammar Geek note: the verbs here — *get, subscribe, download* — are in the imperative mood, i.e. they're giving the reader a command or order.)

Sometimes it helps to adopt the user's voice. Rather than using the words *you* or *your*, try phrasing your CTA from the user's perspective, e.g.:

Send me my tender health check

Rush me my sales report

Show me my heat map
(site on eye-movement stats to detect
image preferences)

WHERE DO USERS GO WHEN THEY CLICK?

When designing an online CTA, be clear about where the user goes when they click on it.

A 'landing page' is the first page of your site that a visitor lands on from an external link. It could be your home page, or any other page on your site. When I write a blog about how to boost bid win-rates, for instance, my CTA contains a link not to my home page, which talks about *all* my services, but to a page dealing specifically with that topic. It's my landing page for that particular link.

Alternatively, you might want your visitor to arrive at a 'squeeze' page. This type of web page focuses on an offer for one product or service only. It's all about the ONE action you want the visitor to take when they land on that page, e.g. buying something or opting in to a list. Its purpose is to 'squeeze' that action out of the visitor. That's why squeeze pages typically have few design elements, i.e. no navigation bar or other links, because they don't want to distract the reader from that goal.

Squeeze pages offer users a binary choice: 'either act or leave'.

GETTING PEOPLE TO TAKE ACTION ON SOCIAL MEDIA

Dan Zarrella, author of *The Science of Marketing*, has done extensive research into what he terms social calls-to-action.

Analysing over 50,000 blog posts, he found that posts containing the words *comment, link* or *share* got more comments, views or links than those that did not.

On Twitter, Zarrella analysed a dataset of millions of tweets. He found that the phrases *please retweet, please rt, please help, spread* and *visit* led to more retweets than tweets that did not use those phrases.

On Facebook, he collected all the posts of the top 10,000 most-liked pages and found that the pages that contained a specific CTA like *share, comment* and *like* got more of the action they requested.

In other words — at least on social media — tell the reader what you want them to do and many will comply.

SIMPLE CTAS IN BASHO EMAILS

Created by Jeff Hoffman, the BASHO email method helps to get the attention of busy prospects, with a view to getting a meeting with them. BASHO emails are brutally short (the whole body is visible in both the preview pane and above the fold) and ask the reader for a mini-commitment, such as a 15-minute phone conversation. I recently ran a BASHO email campaign called

'Want to write like *The Economist?*'. The CTA simply asked the recipient to click on a link to my electronic diary:

> *If you'd like to find out more about getting your people to write like 'The Economist', please book a 15-minute call for us to speak by clicking on this link: https://calendly.com/scottkeyser91/15min. (We've also trained a Magic Circle law firm in writing skills for nine years.)*

(My BASHO campaign led to a number of face-to-face meetings with prospects, resulting in sales. The campaign generated an ROI of 450%.)

FOOD FOR THOUGHT

Look at something you recently wrote to persuade someone to do something different: is there a call to action? If so, is it clear what you want them to do and by when? Is it easy for them to do it, or are you asking them to jump through so many hoops that they'll be put off?

And constantly test: compare two versions of an online CTA to see which one works best in terms of click-through and conversion rates. When you find a clear winner, then test it against a new CTA, to continuously improve the effectiveness of your calls to action.

The bottom line: whenever we're persuading somebody to do something they wouldn't have otherwise done if they hadn't read our words, we need to issue a call to action. The clearer and easier it is for them to comply, the likelier they are to do it. By making our offer, recommendation or proposal and its benefits to the reader irresistible — as well as limiting its availability in either time or supply — we make our call to action *compelling*.

SECTION III:
Editing

Write in white heat; edit in cold blood.

Dr Edna Manlapaz, Creative Writing Professor,
Ateneo de Manila University

rhetorica® Technique #18:

Read Your Writing Out Loud (ROL)

This probably sounds like a very simple technique… and you know what? It is.

I can safely say there are few simpler but more effective writing techniques than this one. Strictly speaking it's an editing/ checking technique, but it will improve your drafting, too.

WHY IS ROL SO EFFECTIVE?

ROL slows you down and allows you to judge your tone of voice. After all, we don't read tone of voice, we *hear* it. This auditory aspect of writing is what makes ROL so important, and so effective.

Besides tone of voice, ROL also catches the clumsy phrase or the sentence that runs on and on and on (you'll know, when you start getting breathless).

When we read text to ourselves (aka 'sub-vocalising' or reading under our breath) or scan it, our brains tend to go on auto-pilot and insert what we want to be there or think is there, but which actually isn't. ROL stops that self-deception in its tracks.

It's such a simple technique, so there's no excuse for not doing it. (If you work in an open-plan office and worry about disturbing your colleagues – or making *them* worry about your sanity – then find an empty meeting-room, go for a walk in the park or find a quiet corner in your local coffee shop.)

And if you're responding to a bid or tender, doing a written test or completing an application with long, rambling questions, ROL each question to ensure you understand what it's driving at. That way, you won't mis-read or mis-interpret what you're being asked for.

Listening aloud to what we've written allows us to tune into the words and their likely effect on the reader. It helps us to get on the reader's wavelength.

HOW DO WE USE ROL WHEN TONE OF VOICE REALLY MATTERS?

ROL comes into its own when we have a difficult or delicate message to deliver and we need to get the clarity and tone of voice spot-on. Here's an example.

Imagine that a junior member of your team, John, has been under-performing on an important project. Following his annual appraisal with you, you have to send him an email that delivers the objectives expressed below in F.F.A. (Facts, Feelings, Actions):

What I want John to know...	What I want John to feel...	What I want John to do...
He has under-performed on project XYZ	Remorseful Scared (of the consequences)	Create an action plan to raise his game
The client has complained about him	Motivated (to change)	
This email is a formal warning, based on his recent performance appraisal	Supported	
He has my support to change/improve his performance		

Here are three different versions of the email, all of which I've read out loud to strike the tone of voice I wanted:

VERSION 1 — FORMAL

Your performance appraisal: formal warning
Scott Keyser scott@scottkeyser.com
Sent: Sun 06/05/2014 09:38
To: john@ROL.com

John, further to your annual appraisal on the 3rd May and the client's complaint about you, this is a formal warning under the terms of your contract that your performance on Project XYZ has not attained the standards of service, responsiveness and time-keeping expected of this firm's Associates.

Please develop a structured action plan by mid-day this Friday 17th May to address these issues, which I will review. You need to be aware that if your performance does not improve markedly in the next three months, we will be forced to take disciplinary action against you, which could include terminating your contract.

Scott

You'd probably agree that this version is über-formal and cold, aloof, impersonal and not very motivating for John. I don't know about you, but if I got an email like this I'd probably jump before I was pushed! While it delivers the objective of giving John a formal warning, it probably fails to make him feel supported or to motivate him to change.

VERSION 2 — INFORMAL

Our recent meeting
Scott Keyser scott@scottkeyser.com
Sent: 06/05/2014 09:38
To: john@ROL.com

Hi John, thanks for the meeting with me last week to chat through your annual appraisal.

As I mentioned, I have to give you a formal warning over your recent performance on Project XYZ (it's an HR requirement), especially after the client complained. Consider yourself warned! But I have every confidence you will turn things around.

On that note, my door is always open to you and your colleagues, so feel free to pop in and discuss how to improve your performance. I know you can do it!

Cheers, Scott

This one's chummy, like I'm trying to be John's best mate rather than his boss. The jaunty, breezy style is weak and lacks authority. Ironically it could be as de-motivating for John as Version 1: he may feel little or no compulsion to change his behaviour.

VERSION 3 — NORMAL

Your performance appraisal
Scott Keyser scott@scottkeyser.com
Sent: Sun 06/05/2014 09:38
To: john@ROL.com

Dear John, following your annual appraisal last week, this is a formal warning under the terms of your contract that your performance on Project XYZ has not reached the standards we expect of an Associate. The client's recent complaint about you made this warning inevitable. This is frustrating for me, as I know you are capable of so much more — as you showed on the ABC project. But the motivation and desire to fulfil that potential must come from you.

As I said when we met, I am ready to give you the help and support you need. With that in mind, please draft by early next week an action plan for improving your performance over the next three months, for us to review and finalise together. We can then see how you do against that plan.

The firm is giving you a chance to show me and your team-mates that you can raise your game. Please don't throw it away.

Scott

In this version, I've tried to strike a balance between being firm / authoritative on the one hand and collaborative / supportive on the other. The tone of voice is altogether more measured.

My point is this: when communicating potentially conflicting or difficult messages, we must ROL to check we're getting the tone of voice right and saying what we mean.

FOOD FOR THOUGHT

Find a recent document and picture the reader in your mind's eye. Spend a few moments thinking about them. Read the document out loud and then answer these questions:

- How might your words have sounded to the reader and made them *feel*? (Remember the oft-neglected Feelings in F.F.A.)

- How would you describe your tone of voice?

- Were your words as clear to your reader as they are to you?

- Have you varied the rhythm of your text, or is it a bit monotonous, or even dull?

- Would you change anything after ROL?

The bottom line: every professional writer does ROL. And so should you.

Here's a quick reminder of the technique:

Read Out Loud.

rhetorica® Technique #19:

Score Your Readability

You close your document with a neat turn of phrase, tap the full-stop key with a flourish, lift your hands from the keyboard and sit back smugly.

But how do you know that what you've written is clear, concise and readable?

You've read it back to yourself over and over, it sounds OK, but you're so close to it you're not the best judge. The deadline is looming. You need objective feedback on it and now.

Enter the Readability Statistics.

Developed by Dr Rudolf Flesch — a Viennese Jew who fled to the US from Nazi persecution and became a New York sociologist famed for his work on readability — this is a little-known function in every version of Microsoft® Word, Outlook and Apple. Here's what it looks like:

Readability Statistics [X]

Counts
Words   766
Characters   3399
Paragraphs   38
Sentences   60

Averages
Sentences per Paragraph   3
Words per Sentence   10.8
Characters per Word   4.1

Readability
Passive Sentences   5%
Flesch Reading Ease   75.6
Flesch-Kincaid Grade Level   5.4

[OK]

It not only gives you standard stuff like word and character count; it also gives you four ratios to aim for:

ASL (Average Sentence Length)	In the middle ('Averages') section, your 'Words per Sentence' is the average number of words per sentence, or ASL. Your ASL heavily influences readability, as long sentences contain more ideas and demand more processing power than short ones. (Technique #20 shows you some easy ways to shorten your sentences.) **Your ASL target: 15–20 words.**
Passive Sentences	In the lower ('Readability') section, 'Passive Sentences' is the proportion of sentences in the passive voice. Passivitis is a chronic affliction (see Technique #15). Writing in the passive voice is longer, less direct and less vigorous than the active voice (the clue's in the name). **Your 'Passive Sentences' target: as close to 0% as possible.**
Flesch Reading Ease (FRE) score	In the same section of the stats, your FRE scores the readability of your text as a percentage, so the higher the better. Dr Flesch used two measures of readability: the average number of words per sentence and average number of syllables per word. In his system, plain English starts at 60% FRE. Authors of technical documents rarely reach those dizzy heights, because technical jargon tends to be polysyllabic, depressing readability. But we should be able to score 45–50% FRE by offsetting techie text with simple supporting language. **Your FRE target: at least 45%.**

Flesch-Kincaid Grade Level	This is functional reading age as measured by the US grade school system, i.e. the minimum amount of American education required to understand a piece of writing.
	To convert Flesch-Kincaid Grade Level into age, add five, i.e. a grade level of 5.0 is roughly an American ten-year-old. This means that, at a minimum, an American ten-year-old could understand your text. It doesn't mean you're targeting that age group!
	No target for this one, but most of my corporate clients set a Flesch-Kincaid Grade Level for their external communications of 10–11. (Recently tested articles from *The Economist* scored an average Flesch-Kincaid level of 10.3 to 10.8, exploding the myth that *The Economist* is high-brow and only for college graduates.)

Word of warning: the stats work best on fully punctuated body copy of at least 200 words; they don't work well on titles, headlines, subheadings, bullet points and captions. If your document has lots of these, save it as a text-only file and run the stats on that for a truer score.

To score your readability, follow two simple steps: 1) activate the stats; 2) run the Spelling & Grammar check.

ACTIVATING THE READABILITY STATS IN MICROSOFT® WORD

Click on 'File' in the toolbar, 'Options' in the left-hand column, then on 'Proofing'. The dialogue box that appears looks like this:

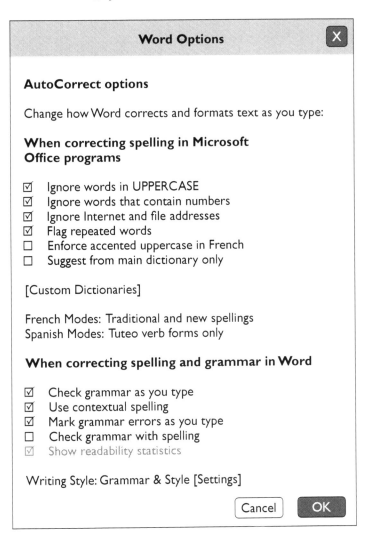

Towards the bottom, under the heading 'When correcting spelling and grammar in Word', are two options: 'Check grammar with spelling', and 'Show readability statistics', which is greyed out. To activate the stats, tick/check the 'Check grammar with spelling' option. The 'Show readability statistics' option below it should then automatically be ticked/checked; if not, do it manually.

Make sure as well that the drop-down box alongside 'Writing Style' says 'Grammar & Style' (as above), and not 'Grammar only'.

To score the readability of your text: put the cursor at the start of your body copy or highlight the text you want to score. Run the Spelling & Grammar check, accepting or rejecting the options as you wish (click on 'Ignore rule' to get through them quickly). At the end of the S & G check, a dialogue box asks if you wish to check the remainder of the document — click 'No' and the readability stats appear.

ACTIVATING THE READABILITY STATS IN MICROSOFT® OUTLOOK

Click on the 'File' tab in the toolbar, 'Options' in the left-hand column, then 'Mail' in the left-hand column, then on 'Spelling and Autocorrect' on the right of the box. You should then get the same dialogue box as shown above: follow the same procedure to activate the stats and apply them to your email text.

ACTIVATING THE READABILITY STATS IN MICROSOFT® WORD FOR MAC 2011

In the toolbar under 'Word', go into 'Preferences': under 'Authoring and Proofing Tools', click on 'Spelling and Grammar'. You should then see this screen:

Spelling and Grammar ▢X

Spelling _____

☑ Check spelling as you type
☐ Hide spelling errors in this document
☑ Always suggest corrections
☐ Suggest from main dictionary only

☑ Use German post-reform rules
☐ Enforce accepted uppercase in French
☐ Russian: Enforce strict e

☑ Ignore words in Uppercase
☑ Ignore words with numbers
☑ Ignore Internet and Files addresses
☑ Flag repeated words

French Modes: Traditional and new spellings
Spanish Modes: Tuteo verb forms only
Portuguese Modes: Post-reform
Brazilian Modes: Post-reform

Custom dictionary: Custom Dictionary

Grammar _____

☑ Check grammar as you type
☐ Show grammatical errors in Notebook Layout View
☐ Hide grammatical errors in this document
☑ Check grammar with spelling
☑ Show readability statistics
  Writing style: Standard

[Cancel] ▮ OK ▮

Tick/check the box marked 'Show readability statistics' and make sure that the 'Writing style' drop-down box says 'Standard'. Click 'OK' and you've activated the stats.

SCORING YOUR READABILITY IN THE ABOVE PROGRAMS

Place the cursor at the start of your body copy or highlight the text you want to score. Run the Spelling & Grammar check ('Tools', in the toolbar), accepting or rejecting the options as you wish (click on 'Ignore' or 'Ignore rule' to get through them quickly). At the end of the S & G check, a dialogue box asks if you wish to check the remainder of the document – click 'No' and the readability stats appear.

TROUBLE-SHOOTING PROBLEMS IN THE READABILITY STATS FEATURE

If you get odd scores (0% readability doesn't mean you're a bad writer!), it may be because…

… your document has lots of graphs, graphics or bullets (the stats work best on body copy/narrative text, i.e. prose of complete, punctuated sentences);

… your word count is too low: the stats struggle with text of fewer than 200 words;

… when you activated the stats in the dialogue box shown above, you should have opted for 'Grammar & Style' in the 'Writing Style' drop-down box, rather than 'Grammar only' (otherwise the 'Show readability statistics' option may be greyed out).

Assessing a piece of writing can be subjective; the readability stats make it more objective. If you're editing contributions to any document, you can now defend your editing decisions with authority. And if your version turns out to be more readable than your boss's, then you face an interesting dilemma…

DON'T LET THE TAIL WAG THE DOG

When I show people on my training courses how to use these readability stats, they run around like frisky puppies editing their work to edge their FRE score over the magic 60% plain English line and beat their colleagues. I like to see healthy competition, but don't let your new-found toy blind you to its limits. The stats only tell you what's going on in your writing *mechanically*; they don't assess the quality of your *content*.

You could be writing complete rubbish; you'll only know that it's readable rubbish.

What I want to cultivate in you, rather, is your writerly judgment, your ability to assess your own writing. If you're happy with what you've written and reckon it hits the spot as far as your reader goes, then whether it scores 59% or 61% is immaterial.

ANOTHER READABILITY FORMULA: THE GUNNING FOG INDEX

Invented in the 1940s by Robert Gunning, an American textbook publisher, the Fog Index is one of the earliest readability formulae. A pioneer of readability research, Gunning believed that newspapers and business documents were full of 'fog' and unnecessary complexity. He founded the first consulting firm specialising in readability, helping the editors and journalists of 60 newspapers and magazines to write for their readers.

Here's how to calculate your Fog Index score:

1. Calculate your ASL (number of words divided by the number of sentences).

2. Calculate the number of words with three or more syllables as a percentage of the total number of words.

3. Add 1. and 2. together, and multiply the total by 0.4.

The result is your Gunning Fog Index, a rough measure of how many years' schooling it would take someone to understand the content. The lower the number, the more understandable the content.

The ideal score is seven or eight; anything above twelve is considered too hard for most readers. The Bible and Mark Twain score around six, while publications like *Time, Newsweek* and *The Wall Street Journal* average around 11.

The Gunning Fog Index reinforces what I've been saying throughout this book: that short sentences written in plain English are easier to understand than long sentences written in complicated language. If you find your Index soaring into the teens, you've lost most of your readers in the dense fog of your writing.

Finally, here are the readability stats on this chapter:

Readability Statistics	X
Counts	
Words	1191
Characters	5773
Paragraphs	38
Sentences	49
Averages	
Sentences per Paragraph	3
Words per Sentence	20.5
Characters per Word	4.6
Readability	
Passive Sentences	0%
Flesch Reading Ease	59.3
Flesch-Kincaid Grade Level	9.7
	OK

My ASL is OK at 20.5 words, I have no symptoms of passivitis with 0% passive sentences, and my FRE score shows that I'm less than one percentage point shy of plain English. (I know, I know: teacher's pet comes to mind.)

FOOD FOR THOUGHT

Print out a recent document or communication and read it out loud.

Does it say what you wanted it to say?

Now you're happy with the content, score its readability and pay attention to the four key numbers:

1. ASL

2. Proportion of sentences in the passive voice

3. FRE (Flesch Reading Ease), aka readability out of 100

4. Flesch-Kincaid Grade Level

The bottom line: assessing your or someone else's writing can be highly subjective. The readability stats take much of the subjectivity out of it and show us what's going on mechanically in the text. And if we're coaching someone on their writing, the stats allow us to give them evidence-based feedback.

For a bonus, here are five easy ways to raise your FRE score:

1. Simplify your language with plain English.

2. Turn your passive sentences into active ones.

3. Shorten your sentences (next chapter).

4. Use more verbs than nouns.

5. Keep technical jargon to a minimum.

rhetorica® Technique #20:

Shorten Your Sentences

One of the most common writing issues I come across is long sentences.

Long sentences are an issue because they usually contain multiple ideas, so they're more taxing on the reader's brain than short sentences. You're forcing the reader to hold more ideas in their head till they get to the full-stop and complete their understanding of your message. In computer terms, they're having to hold more bits in their cache memory.

Research shows that 50% of readers get lost if a sentence exceeds 14 words, but a whacking 80% get lost if it exceeds 20 words. Long, complicated sentences do not impress your reader; they just irritate them.

On the other hand, you don't want to be writing über-short sentences that patronise your reader with Janet & John-style copy, like:

> *We are launching a new initiative. It will be a priority for us. It will be based in Manchester. We will be putting many resources behind it. We hope you will support it.*

This choppy, staccato style doesn't flow and is hard to read. There's a balance to strike between long and short sentences and that's where average sentence length (ASL) comes in.

Across the board of your writing, your ASL should be 15–20 words. Some of your sentences will be 27 words long, others will be eight, but as long as the average falls within the range of 15–20, you're good to go.

If you read the previous chapter, you will know that the readability stats calculate your ASL for you. The two measures of readability that the stats use are average words per sentence and average number of syllables per word. Longer average sentences lower readability.

FIVE WAYS TO WRITE SHORTER SENTENCES

1. Omit needless words.

2. Turn your passive sentences into active ones.

3. Create new sentences out of *which* clauses.

4. Find the FANBOYS (*for, and, nor, but, or, yet, so*) conjunctions — joining words — and insert a full-stop immediately before them. Then make a new sentence beginning with the conjunction (yes, you can do that: forget what you were told at school).

5. Use this punctuation mark a lot: .

In the following example, I've underlined the conjunctions *so* and *but*, and the relative pronoun *which*:

> **Version A.** *We work proactively with clients and local authorities to protect trees, flora and fauna and other*

habitats close to or within demolition projects, so wild-life surveys of bats, badgers and other protected species can be carried out prior to the commencement of works on a major project. One project was delayed for more than six months while a bat colony was allowed time to find another roost, which added a further £5m to the budget, but this is now, in the environmentally aware times we live in, what the public expects.

Readability stats: word count, 90; ASL, 45 words; FRE, 29.5%.

Let's see what happens when we put a full-stop before each underlined word, begin the next sentence with that word or remove it altogether, and replace *which* with *This*:

Version B. *We work proactively with clients and local authorities to protect trees, flora and fauna and other habitats close to or within demolition projects. We ensure that wildlife surveys of bats, badgers and other protected species are carried out prior to the commencement of works on a major project. One project was delayed for more than six months while a bat colony was allowed time to find another roost. This added a further £5m to the budget. But in the environmentally aware times we live in, this is now what the public expects.*

Readability stats: word count, 91; ASL, 18.2 words; FRE, 56.3%.

By changing only three things in this passage, we've brought the ASL down to within the ideal range of 15–20 words and gained almost 27 percentage points readability.

Now let's see what happens when we also tighten up the text by omitting needless words and simplifying some of the language:

> **Version C.** *We work closely with clients and local authorities to protect natural habitats in or near demolition projects. We carry out surveys of bats, badgers and other protected species before every major project. One project was delayed for more than six months to let a bat colony find another roost. This added £5m to the budget. But this is now what the environmentally aware public expects.*
>
> **Readability stats: word count, 66; ASL, 13 words; FRE, 54.3%.**

As you can see, Version C is much shorter with a 27% cut in word count (66 vs 91) and an even lower ASL. We've lost a couple of percentage points in readability, but I suspect that's because the readability stats algorithm is spooked by the low number of words (the stats work best on a minimum of 200 words).

Another way of describing what we did above is that we 'separated independent clauses from subordinate clauses'. In the sentence, *'One project was delayed for more than six months while a bat colony was allowed time to find another roost,* **which added a further £5m to the budget**', the main or independent clause is the one in italics. The clause in bold is technically known as a 'non-defining or non-restrictive' relative clause.

If you're not familiar with these grammar terms, don't panic!

The clause in italics gives the main message and is *independent* because you could put a full-stop after *roost* and the sentence would still make sense. It could stand on its own.

The bold relative clause, however, is secondary to the main clause because it gives additional but non-essential information about the project delay. Of course, a relative clause beginning *which* isn't a complete sentence and can't stand on its own. But if we replace *which* with *This*, then it can. Separating the two clauses results in two new sentences:

> *One project was delayed for more than six months to let a bat colony find another roost. This added £5m to the budget.*

And we've cut the ASL from 28 to 11.5 words.

Think of secondary or relative clauses as mini-sentences. You can remove them from the sentence they are in and, with a few changes, turn them into sentences in their own right — as above.

When we combine a main clause with two or more subordinate clauses as in Version A, we create what are known as *compound sentences*. The more and longer compound sentences you write, the harder your reader will be working to get your meaning.

ÜBER-SHORT SENTENCES CARRY A PUNCH

Short sentences convey authority, confidence and conviction, especially if preceded by a slew of longer ones. Here are some examples:

> *That night she sat on Tom's bed and waited for him to touch her.* **But he didn't.**

> *She moved from Michigan to New York City to kick-start her career as a dancer. She's sold more than 300 million records worldwide and is recognized by Guinness World Records as the best-selling female recording artist of all time. She's turned her hand to acting, winning a Golden Globe Award for Evita. She's been acclaimed as a businesswoman, founding entertainment company Maverick in 1992 as a JV with Time Warner and in 2007 signed an unprecedented $120 million deal with*

Live Nation. **Madonna is the master of reinvention.**

I've tried calling you, emailing you, writing to you, getting introduced through mutual friends, even sky-writing, but still no reply from you or your secretary. **I give up.**

The shortest sentence you can have is a 'sentence fragment'. It can deliver a sarcastic or sardonic twist right at the end, or stand out thanks to its sheer brevity:

Subsistence farmers will stop shooting the cheetahs that kill their cattle because they want to protect an endangered species. As if.

Use phrases and even words as sentences. Really.

Your comments on my work hurt me. A lot.

Man is the only animal that blushes. Or needs to.
(Mark Twain)

FOOD FOR THOUGHT

Fish out a live or recent piece of writing and run the readability stats over it. If your ASL is higher than 15–20 words, your sentences are too long. Separate the main clauses from the secondary ones by identifying the most common conjunctions (e.g. *for, and, nor, but, or, yet, so*) or the relative pronoun *which*. Insert a full-stop immediately before them and start the next sentence with that word, or remove it altogether. Read the new version out loud. Rinse and repeat. (Oh, and remember to omit needless words.)

In this technique I've gone into more detail about grammar than in any other, because I felt it necessary to show you how easy it is to shorten your sentences. But this isn't a book on grammar. There are several excellent English grammar books; I recommend these if you want to delve deeper into the topic:

- *Oxford A–Z of Grammar and Punctuation*, John Seely, OUP

- *Good Punctuation,* Graham King, Collins

- *The Penguin Guide to Punctuation*, RL Trask, Penguin Books

The bottom line: to hold the reader's attention and convey complex information clearly, we need to keep our ASL within the optimal range of 15–20 words. Higher than that and we make our reader work harder than they might want to; lower than that and we risk sounding childish or patronising.

The only other thing you need to do now is proofread your text and banish typos to oblivion... which is your cue for the final rhetorica® Technique #21.

rhetorica® Technique #21:

Banish Typos Forever

When I ask delegates on my writing workshops to rate out of ten the importance of issuing a document without a 'typo' (a typographical error, like a misspelled word), they usually say nine, ten or even 11. After all, if you can't be bothered or don't have the time to proofread your writing, what does that tell your reader about your attitude or process?

I once heard a great analogy for describing the effect on the reader of a typo. Good writing is like looking through a clear window: you're not aware of the glass, only the view. But a typo acts as a smudge on the window. In other words, the typo calls attention to the writing and not the message.

GET YOUR MIND RIGHT

To proofread efficiently, it helps to set the right conditions and the right mental attitude.

It's easier and less tiring for the eyes to proofread printed matter, so print your text out and proofread it in well-lit conditions, ideally with lots of natural light. Checking on screen is both tiring and inefficient.

Proofreading isn't a creative activity, but it does demand focus and concentration, so try to avoid doing it when you're tired. I heard someone say 'Write at night; edit in the morning'. Not bad advice. So draft your text, then sleep on it. Re-visit your text with fresh eyes. Make a clear separation between drafting and editing/proofreading, both physically and mentally. Proofreading is best done *methodically*; it's a marathon, not a sprint. We rush it at our peril. Here are seven proofreading methods that work for me, either solo or in combination:

1. **Read your writing out loud.** I use ROL to check for content, word-choice, tone of voice *and* typos. Refer back to Technique #18 for all the great benefits of ROL.

2. **Run the Spelling & Grammar check.** This is basic and one you probably already use. It catches most typos, but beware: it won't catch words which exist but which don't make sense in the context of your draft, e.g. *sing* when you meant *sign*, *form* when you meant *from*, *cant* when you meant *can't*.

3. **Read backwards[14].** Print out your document. Go to the last word on the last page and read backwards, from right to left and from bottom to top, revealing each preceding line with a piece of card as you work from the back of the document to the front. If you have no card to hand, use your finger: move your finger along the line under each word as you read. This stops your eyes racing ahead of your brain (and works when you're proofreading from left to right, too). Reading backwards destroys the brain's ability to make sense of what you're reading, forcing you to consider one word at a time. It catches what smell-cheek, I mean spell-check, misses: you have enough context from the rest of the line to know whether it should be *sing* or *sign*. It also catches double spaces, duplicated punctuation marks and mis-capitalisation. Most people don't proofread properly. They think that

---

14   LR Communications Systems, blog, 1999; *Write to Sell* (Cyan, 2007)

scanning or skimming over their text is enough, but the risk is that they will read what they want to read, rather than what is actually there. Reading backwards makes that impossible.

4. **Check for one type of error at a time.** List all the error types and/or the parts of your document that you will check for. You'll want to come up with your own, but here are a few suggestions to get you started:

- house style

- body copy

- headings, i.e. headlines, subheadings

- page numbers, accuracy of table of contents, headers, footers

- graphics (+ captions), e.g. images, graphs, tables, charts

- spelling and grammar

- facts and figures

- proper names

- font size, spacing between words, 'leading' (spacing between lines of text)

Go through your text several times, following the order of your list and crossing out each error type as you complete the check. This iterative approach helps the mind focus on and tune into a specific error type in turn, avoiding fatigue and error-blindness.

5. **Print your text out in a different style, leading and/or font.** This can shake your brain out of its comfort zone, bring fresh eyes to the text and avoid the blindness that comes with familiarity.

6. **Get someone else to read it — preferably a professional proofreader!** When we've worked hard on a piece of text, we can get too close to it and not see the wood for the trees. Handing it over to someone who has no attachment to it means they're likelier to catch errors that we've missed in our blind spot. And if they do it for a living, even better.

7. **Make your own proofreading checklist.** Keep a list of the errors you usually make and refer to it every time you proofread. (Thanks to Richard Nordquist for this one.)

FOOD FOR THOUGHT

Using any of the above methods, have a go at proofreading this short piece of text, then check over the page to see how you did:

Our garden is is a disaster. We live in south London, in a semide-tached that used to form part of a huge orchard once owned by the Robertson family, he of jam fame.. A row of trees run in a straight line along the back of our garden, tracing the path of a long-lost stream that, I guess, used to water the fertile orchard. A legacy of of those fruity days is an enormous pear tree that dominates our garden, shields us from the neighbours gaze but throws so much shadow on our lawn that that the grass is patchy at best. The tree also produces giant pears, but because they hang so high up, we cant pick them. So they grow and grow and grow till they're become so plump and fat and heavy that they plummet to earth and splatter all over the lawn, cre-ating sweet brown pear-pats that is Heaven to wasps. My wife and I ask our children to pick them up with rubber gloves, but we have to pay them more than the minimum wage to to do it. And even then they leave half the pear-cake in the grass. In fact, the frist time my daughter did it, she got stung – and doubled her fee. So I guess, even though we don't have the Wembley style lawn that my wife craves, our kids have learnt to be more commerical. You never know: one of them might become the finance director of a food manufacture....making pear jam.

PROOFREADING TEST: FAIR COPY

Our garden **is** a disaster. We live in **S**outh London, in a **semi-detached** that used to form part of a huge orchard once owned by the Robertson family, he of jam fame. A row of trees **runs** in a straight line along the back of our garden, tracing the path of a long-lost stream that, I imagine, used to water the fertile orchard. A legacy **of** those fruity days is an enormous pear tree that dominates our garden, shields us from our **neighbours'** gaze, but throws so much shadow on our lawn **that** the grass is patchy at best. The tree also produces giant pears, but because they hang so high up, we **can't** pick them. So they grow and grow and grow till **they've** become so plump and fat and heavy that **they plummet** to earth and splatter all over the lawn, creating sweet brown pear-pats that is **h**eaven to wasps. My wife and I ask our children to pick them up with rubber gloves, but we have to pay them more than the minimum wage **to** do it. And even then they leave half the clotted pear-cake in the grass. In fact, the **first** time my daughter did it, she got **stung** — **and doubled** her fee. So I guess, even though we don't have the **Wembley-style** lawn that my wife craves, our kids have learnt to be more **commercial**. You never know: one of them might become the Finance **D**irector of a food **manufacturer...** making pear jam.

Answer sheet:

1. Repetition of *is*.

2. *South* is lower case (i.e. south), except when part of a name, e.g. South Africa.

3. Semi-detached (house).

4. Double full-stop.

5. The verb *run* refers to the row, not the trees, so should be *runs* (singular).

6. Repetition of *of*.

7. Add the possessive apostrophe: *neighbours' gaze*, i.e. the gaze of our neighbours.

8. Repetition of *that*.

9. *Can't* vs *cant*.

10. *They,* not *they're*.

11. Double space between *they* and *plummet*.

12. Heaven is lower case.

13. Repetition of *to*.

14. *First,* not *frist*.

15. Use an em-dash (—), not an en-dash (–), and absolutely not a hyphen (-), to give a punchline.

16. Insert a hyphen between *Wembley* and *style*, i.e. a lawn in the style of the Wembley pitch, vs a style lawn (whatever that is!).

17. *Commercial,* not *commerical.*

18. Finance Director is a title or proper noun, so should be upper case.

19. *Manufacturer* (i.e. the maker), not *manufacture* (the making).

20. Ellipsis should only have three points.

You may well have spotted most of these typos reading the text in the normal way, but I wager you will have netted all of them using one of the seven proofreading techniques. And if you're emailing a client or writing the executive summary of a major bid document, you won't want a single typo, will you?

The bottom line: in an age when people are bombarded by words and seek reasons *not* to read them, we mustn't make it easy for them with a careless typo. Do whatever it takes to banish typos. Keep that window smudge-free.

Epilogue

Thank you for reading this book. I sincerely hope that in some small way I've given you more confidence in your writing, so that you can now conquer the world with your words and ideas. If you have any feedback for me, would like to get involved in my mission to change how we teach writing skills to young people across the globe, or you'd like to know more about my writing workshops for corporates and other organisations, please drop me a line at scott@scottkeyser.com.

Alternatively, if you'd like to take your writing to the next level, then check out my online writing programme, rhetorica® Online, at www.writeforresults.com.

And finally, if you just want to stay in touch and get regular communications tips, then sign up for my monthly newsletter at www.writeforresults.com.

Good luck with your writing!

Bibliography

Barker, Alan. *Improve your Communication Skills*. Kogan Page, 2010.

Bragg, Melvyn. *The Adventure of English*. Sceptre, 2003.

Camp, Lindsay. *Can I change your mind?* Bloomsbury, 2007.

Charvet, Shelle Rose. *Words That Change Minds*. Kendall/Hunt Publishing, 1995.

Cialdini, Robert; Goldstein, Noah; Martin, Steve. *Yes! 50 secrets from the science of persuasion*. Profile Books, 2007.

Crystal, David. *Words Words Words*. Oxford University Press, 2006.

Forsyth, Mark. *The Elements of Eloquence*. Icon Books, 2013.

Fowler, Alastair. *How To Write*. Oxford University Press, 2006.

Graves, Robert; Hodge, Alan. *The Reader Over Your Shoulder*. Vintage Books, 1979.

Leith, Sam. *You Talkin' To Me?* Profile Books, 2012.

Maslen, Andy. *Write to Sell: the Ultimate Guide to Great Copywriting.* Cyan, 2007.

Morris, Rupert. *The Right Way to Write.* Piatkus, 1998.

Seely, John. *Oxford A–Z of Grammar & Punctuation.* Oxford University Press, 2013.

Strunk, William Jr; White, Elwyn Brooks. *The Elements of Style.* Longman, 1999.

The Economist Style Guide: The Bestselling Guide to English Usage. Profile Books, 2010.

Truss, Lynne. *Eats, Shoots & Leaves.* Profile Books, 2005.

Waterhouse, Keith. *English Our English (and how to sing it).* Viking, 1991.

The Author

Scott Keyser is The Writing Guy™.

Trainer, consultant and coach, Scott helps professional services firms around the world produce written communications that are clear, concise, compelling, confident and convincing.

His career includes stints at J Walter Thompson, Saatchi & Saatchi, PricewaterhouseCoopers and Ernst & Young (now EY). He trained staff of an international weekly news magazine in writing skills for ten years and helped one of the Big Four accountancy firms to double its tender win-rate.

Now he shows other high calibre organisations — including Magic Circle law firms — how easy it is to write well and get a better return on their investment in the written word. Even tough Texan oil & gas engineers have been moved to tears by the tectonic shift in their writing.

Thought leadership pieces, blogs, articles, client alerts, news-letters, sales letters, emails, reports, business cases, appraisals, bids, tenders, pitches, proposals — all can be improved with his rhetorica® techniques.

Writing is a life skill and Scott has solved the riddle of how to do it well.
http://www.scottkeyser.com
www.twitter.com/scottkeyser
https://uk.linkedin.com/in/scottkeyser1

31017620R00139

Printed in Great Britain
by Amazon